FUNDAMENTALS OF THE SECURITIES INDUSTRY

WILLIAM A. RINI

McGraw-Hill

New York   Chicago   San Francisco
Lisbon   London   Madrid   Mexico City
Milan   New Delhi   San Juan   Seoul
Singapore   Sydney   Toronto

Library of Congress Cataloging-in-Publication Data
Rini, William A.
   Fundamentals of the securities industry / William A. Rini.
      p. cm.
   Includes index.
     ISBN 0-07-140318-3
      1. Securities industry.   2. Securities industry—United States.
    3. Securities.   4. Securities—United States.   I. Title.
     HG4521 .R538 2003
     332.63'2—dc21

2002005974

McGraw-Hill

*A Division of The **McGraw-Hill** Companies*

1 2 3 4 5 6 7 8 9 0   QPD/QPD   0 9 8 7 6 5 4 3 2

ISBN 0-07-140318-3

McGraw-Hill books are available at special quantity discounts to use as premiums and sales promotions, or for use in corporate training programs. For more information, please write to the Director of Special Sales, Professional Publishing, McGraw-Hill, Two Penn Plaza, New York, NY 10121-2298. Or contact your local bookstore.

This publication is designed to provide accurate and authoritative information in regard to the subject matter covered. It is sold with the understanding that neither the author nor the publisher is engaged in rendering legal, accounting, futures/securities trading, or other professional service. If legal advice or other expert assistance is required, the services of a competent professional person should be sought.

—From a Declaration of Principles jointly adopted by a Committee
of the American Bar Association and a Committee of Publishers

This book is printed on recycled, acid-free paper containing a minimum of 50 percent recycled, de-inked fiber.

For our dear friends, Ralph and Anita Chirico

Contents

Introduction

This book was written to provide interested parties with an overview of the principal financial products—common and preferred stocks; rights and warrants; corporate, government, and municipal bonds; mutual funds and stock options—and how they are created (the primary market) and traded (the secondary market). It is a primer on stocks, bonds, and options designed for those relatively new to the financial services industry and for those who might benefit from learning "Wall Street's" basics, for professional or private purposes.

This book will serve as a primer about securities, the book you study before moving on to higher-level training materials. This is where you start to learn about "the market." I have attempted to explore each of the subjects in just enough detail to give you a general knowledge of the area—enough knowledge and background so that you can be better prepared to read the financial press and to study more targeted texts in the future.

Unlike many reference works, this book is designed to be read in its entirety, from first page to last page, in order, as many of the concepts build on each other. It explains many of the market's buzzwords, including margin calls, earnings per share, yield to maturity, accrued interest, short sale, ex-dividend, puts and calls, and many other financial terms—all at a basic level. Each of the 20 chapters is supported by a 5-question multiple-choice quiz and a set of exercises to ensure that you understand the chapter contents. The answers (fully detailed) are provided as well.

WILLIAM A. RINI

Acknowledgments

Many thanks to my more than patient editors, advisors, and mentors, Philip Ruppel, Stephen Isaacs, Fred Dahl, and Bob Gulick. And *all* thanks to my dear wife Catherine.

CHAPTER 1

The Corporation

The study of stocks and the stock market must necessarily begin with defining what stocks are. Stocks are *equity* securities, signifying that the owners of such securities have an equity (ownership) position—a "piece of the action"—in a corporation. The two principal types of stocks are common stock and preferred stock. The first five chapters of this text deal with equity securities.

Bonds are *debt* securities. The bondholder has loaned money to the enterprise (corporation or government) and has a debtor–creditor relationship with the issuer of the bonds rather than an ownership interest. Chapters 6 through 10 deal with bonds.

Specialized types of packaged securities marketed by *investment companies* are described in Chapter 11. Such funds may have portfolios composed, at least in part, of stocks or bonds.

The world of puts and calls is addressed in Chapters 12, 13, and 14. These *options* represent the right to buy and sell stocks at prearranged prices.

Chapters 15 through 19 explore how stocks and bonds are brought to the market (the primary market) and how they are subsequently traded (the secondary market): how investors actually buy and sell securities, types of orders, short selling, and margin trading.

The final chapter deals with the analysis of securities—the science (art?) of selecting securities for inclusion in one's investment portfolio, and the timing of purchases and sales.

We begin with how a stock is "born."

SOLE PROPRIETORSHIPS

Most businesses start as small companies owned by a single individual. These are known as *sole proprietorships*, the formal name for businesses owned by just one person. He or she keeps all the profits—that's the good news—but is also responsible for all the losses. Such businesses have to be concerned with only a minimum of paperwork, but might find it difficult to raise capital for expansion.

PARTNERSHIPS

Sometimes, as the little business starts to grow, the single owner joins with other people (partners) to help run the company. These people work together as a *partnership*. Many medium-size companies are partnerships. Both sole proprietorships and partnerships use part of their profits for expansion, sometimes adding their own savings or borrowing money from banks. Many banks, particularly commercial banks, make short-term loans to businesses; but they are usually unwilling to lend such businesses money for long periods of time, so companies traditionally borrow from banks only for their short-term needs.

The growth of both sole proprietorships and partnerships may be limited because they might find it difficult to borrow money that they will be able to repay quickly. It takes a lot of money and a lot of time to build facilities such as new factories or offices. These new facilities may take many years to become profitable, so money borrowed to build them cannot ordinarily be repaid for some time. One of the benefits of becoming a corporation is that it is much easier for a corporation to raise money for expansion, money that will not have to be repaid soon after it is borrowed. This is one of the important reasons that corporations are formed.

Both sole proprietorships and partnerships have other weaknesses as well. They cease to exist when the sole proprietor or a partner dies. There are exceptions to this, but neither form of business is said to have "continuity of existence." This can be very awkward for a thriving business established as a sole proprietorship or partnership, as the company might suffer large losses due to the untimely death of the boss or a major partner. Another risk is that sole proprietors and partners can be sued for their private assets as well as for their interests in the business. Not only are they at risk for whatever investment they have in the company, but they might also lose their savings and other outside investments, assets that have nothing to do with the business.

CORPORATIONS

Becoming a *corporation* addresses the drawbacks of sole proprietorships and partnerships. Corporations can own property; have continuity of existence (so they keep on going despite the death of one or more of the officers and directors); can sue or be sued (but the owners of the corporation can lose only what they have invested—their other assets are not at risk); are legal entities considered to be "artificial persons"; can incur debts; and can raise capital fairly easily by selling shares of stock (giving investors part ownership) or bonds (borrowing from investors). Almost all businesses that are successful eventually become corporations for some or all of these reasons.

State of Incorporation

Every corporation has to have a home state. It is said to be *incorporated* in that state. A company must apply to the Secretary of State at one of the 50 state capitals. It might choose to incorporate by applying to Albany, New York or Trenton, New Jersey or Sacramento, California; but quite a number choose to incorporate in Dover, the capital of the state of Delaware. Delaware is a popular home state because it has very liberal policies, permitting companies incorporated there fairly wide latitude. For this reason, about 40% of large U.S. corporations are incorporated in Delaware, even though they may not conduct their actual business within that state or have any factories or showrooms there.

Corporate Charter

A company wishing to become a corporation (to incorporate) must submit its articles of incorporation to the state of its choosing. This document might be considered the company's constitution. It lists fairly detailed information about the corporation-to-be, including the names of all the directors, a description of the business the company is engaged in, where its facilities are located, its major customers, its audited financial statements, its capitalization, and other essential facts. After the state approves the articles of incorporation, a certificate of incorporation is issued which, together with the articles of incorporation, becomes the company's *charter*. The charter is very much like a license to operate as a corporation, and it also contains the rules under which the company will be operated.

Board of Directors

A corporation is run by a group of people known as a *board of directors*. There are usually between 6 and 12 directors for the average-size corporation. Each of the directors is said to have a "seat" on the board. The chief director is known as the chairman of the board and is the corporation's highest-ranking person. The board members see to it that the corporation is operated in accordance with both the corporate charter and the *bylaws* that govern the company's internal management. Sometimes the members of the board of directors are also officers of the corporation such as president, vice president, or secretary; sometimes some or all of these directors are not officers of the corporation and are then known as outside directors. Directors are elected by the common shareholders, usually for a term of one year. The directors choose the company's officers.

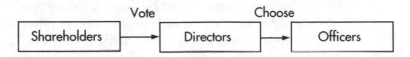

Authorized and Outstanding Shares of Common Stock

A corporation must issue certificates known as "shares of common stock." These certificates—common stock certificates—represent ownership in the corporation. Those who own this stock are part owners of the corporation. The corporation will be given permission by the Secretary of State of the state in which it is incorporated to issue (sell) a certain number of shares of common stock. The shares the company is given permission to sell are the *authorized* shares. Any authorized shares that are sold or otherwise distributed (issued) are then known as *outstanding* shares. Authorized shares that are not sold initially are called "authorized but unissued" shares and may be issued by the corporation at a later time.

Treasury Stock

Sometimes a company may repurchase some of its outstanding stock from shareholders. Such stock is known as *treasury stock*. Treasury stock is authorized (the company had to have permission to sell it in the first place), is considered to be issued because it was once sold (once issued, always issued), but is no longer outstanding.

> **Stock that was sold to investors and that investors still own is** *authorized,* **issued,** **and** *outstanding.*
>
> **Stock that the company never sold in the first place (after it was authorized) is** *authorized but unissued.*
>
> **Issued stock that was repurchased by the company (treasury stock) is** *authorized and issued, but not outstanding.*

A company therefore has two sources of stock to sell: authorized but unissued stock (stock that has never been issued) and treasury stock (issued but repurchased stock). Once it has exhausted these two sources, it cannot issue any more stock unless the common stockholders specifically approve such action.

Equity Securities

All U.S. corporations have common stock outstanding, and the individuals and institutions that own the outstanding stock are the owners of the corporations. Common stocks are *equity* (ownership) securities. If 1,000 shares of a corporation's common stock are outstanding and you own 50 of those shares, then you own 5% of the company. Your 50 shares represent 5% of the total number of shares outstanding (50 divided by 1,000 = .05, or 5%). Of course, most large corporations have millions of common shares outstanding, so that even if you own several hundred shares you will own only a tiny percentage of the company, certainly much less than a fraction of 1%.

Par Value

Common stocks have their *par value* set by the issuing corporation. It is usually a low figure, $1 or less, that has no direct relationship to the stock's original offering price, its current price, its book value, or its dividend policy. Some companies assign a "no par" value to their common shares. Par value *is* important when dealing with preferred stocks (another type of equity security) and bonds.

SUMMARY

A corporation is a company, usually a fairly large one, that has been chartered by a state (or sometimes by the federal government) to conduct its business. It has continuous existence. It is managed by a board of directors elected by the shareholders, and sometimes also by officers selected by the board. The corporation has issued shares of common stock, an equity security, which represent ownership in the corporation.

Corporations can raise money by selling their shares of common stock to individuals and to institutions such as banks and insurance companies (investors) who want to profit from their investment. Those who purchase stock in a company are considered part owners of that corporation; those who purchase the company's bonds are considered to have loaned money to the company.

At the end of each chapter in this book you will find a multiple-choice quiz and a set of practice exercises. We suggest that you work through all the questions in turn, then check your answers with the answers provided. Pay particular attention to the explanations, because they repeat many of the more important teaching points covered in the chapter and often include material not covered in the chapter itself.

MULTIPLE-CHOICE QUIZ

1. Businesses usually borrow money, short-term, from:
    a. insurance companies
    b. mutual funds
    c. savings banks
    d. commercial banks

2. One of the advantages of becoming a corporation is that:
    a. taxes are lower
    b. it is easier to obtain long-term financing
    c. you are guaranteed to make money
    d. directors cannot be fired

3. A company's charter consists of its:
    a. cash and common stock
    b. factories and offices
    c. certificate and articles of incorporation
    d. books and records for the past 10 years

4. A corporation's highest-ranking person is its:
    a. president
    b. oldest director
    c. largest stockholder
    d. chairman of the board

5. Common stock represents _____ in a corporation.
    a. liability
    b. ownership
    c. employment
    d. speculation

PRACTICE EXERCISES

The XYZ Corporation has 2,500,000 authorized common shares. Of these shares, 2,000,000 have been issued and 1,800,000 are outstanding. The Ironworkers' Retirement Fund owns 250,000 common shares of the XYZ Corporation.

1. Does XYZ have any treasury stock? If so, how many shares?

2. How many additional shares may XYZ distribute?

3. What percentage of the XYZ Corporation does the Ironworkers' Retirement Fund own?

MULTIPLE-CHOICE ANSWERS AND EXPLANATIONS

1. **d.** Businesses traditionally borrow from commercial banks for their short-term needs. The larger, better known corporations with good credit ratings are usually able to borrow at the *prime rate*, the lowest rate available. Individuals are generally charged much higher rates of interest. Businesses satisfy their long-term cash needs by selling common stock and other securities to investors.

2. **b.** This was explained in the answer to question 1. Corporations pay fairly high taxes on their earnings, about 35%. Companies are not guaranteed to make money and every year hundreds of businesses fail. Directors are usually elected for a one-year term and there is no guarantee that they will be reelected.

3. **c.** The founders of a corporation file articles of incorporation with a state. After approval, the state issues a certificate of incorporation. A company's charter is made up of both documents and gives the corporation its legal existence. The company's bylaws govern its internal management.

4. **d.** The chairman of the board is a corporation's highest-ranking person. In actual practice, someone else may have more authority. The person with the most decision-making clout is known as the chief executive officer (CEO). Sometimes the chairman is the CEO, sometimes not.

5. **b.** Common stock represents ownership in a corporation. Common stock is an equity security. Those who own the common stock own the corporation. There are other types of equity securities, such as preferred stocks, which are discussed later in this book.

ANSWERS TO PRACTICE EXERCISES

1. The XYZ Corporation has 200,000 shares of treasury stock.

   This can be calculated by subtracting the outstanding shares from the issued shares (2,000,000 − 1,800,000 = 200,000). These reacquired shares cannot vote, nor do they receive dividends. Only outstanding shares are used to calculate earnings per share and book value, thus both these amounts are affected when a company repurchases some of its common stock. Treasury stock can be used for any worthwhile corporate purpose, including resale in the open market.

2. The XYZ Corporation may distribute as many as 700,000 shares.

   It still has available 500,000 of the shares it was authorized to issue as well as the 200,000 shares of treasury stock.

3. The Fund owns 13.9% of the XYZ Corporation.

   The Retirement Fund's percentage of ownership is found by dividing the number of shares of common stock it owns by the total number of common shares outstanding: 250,000 / 1,800,000 = 13.9%.

Common Stock

All corporations issue common stock. Most companies issue only one kind of common stock, but sometimes a company may have several different classes of common stock outstanding at the same time. Most companies issue common stock that carries the right to vote (voting stock); some few companies issue only non-voting stock, while others may issue several different kinds of stock, class A and class B, for example, only one of which carries the right to vote. Shareholders vote for their choice of directors and are also asked to approve a number of matters that may be beyond the ordinary day-to-day decisions made by the company's officers and directors. Shareholders must approve such extraordinary issues as mergers, stock splits, name changes, or dramatic shifts in the nature of the company's core business.

CUMULATIVE AND STATUTORY VOTING

There are two primary voting systems, *statutory* voting and *cumulative* voting. Statutory voting, by far the most common, permits stockholders to cast one vote for every share that they own (e.g., one vote per share for each director running for election). If there are 5 different seats to be filled, the owner of 100 shares of stock could cast a maximum of 100 votes for each of the 5 different directors, for a total of 500 votes, but no more than 100 votes for any single director. Under cumulative voting, the shareholder can save some or all of the votes and cast them for just a few directors, or for only one director. Confused? Here's an example:

Let's assume that there are two different factions vying for each director's seat, the good guys and the bad guys. There are a total of 650 voting shares outstanding; 500 of those shares are owned by stockholders friendly with the bad guys and the other 150 shares are owned by stockholders who like the good guys. Each faction has a representative on the ballot for each of the five open positions, as shown in the table, and the company uses statutory voting.

	Seat 1	Seat 2	Seat 3	Seat 4	Seat 5
Bad Guys	Samuel	Alice	John	Theresa	Bob
	vs.	vs.	vs.	vs.	vs.
Good Guys	Carol	Ted	Cathy	Maria	Beth

Those owning the 500 shares (the bad guys) all vote for their bad-guy buddies, while the good guys owning only 150 shares vote for *their* favorites. The vote totals will look like this:

Bad Guys	Samuel	Alice	John	Theresa	Bob
Number of Votes	500	500	500	500	500

Good Guys	Carol	Ted	Cathy	Maria	Beth
Number of Votes	150	150	150	150	150

The bad guys won every seat! Under statutory voting, those owning a majority of the voting stock will win every voting contest. Those with more than 50% of the voting stock will thus have 100% control. Some people have no argument with this situation (especially those who own or control more than 50% of the voting shares), but it really is not fair that stockholders having a sizable minority position cannot elect at least one of their own. This situation is partially remedied under the cumulative voting system. This system permits shareholders to split their votes whichever way they choose to. They can withhold votes entirely from some of the candidates and save them for one or more of the other candidates. Let's redo the vote we just analyzed, this time under cumulative voting.

The good guys have decided to put all their voting power behind Cathy and not even try to elect their other four candidates. They saved all their votes for Cathy and cast none for Carol, Ted, Maria, or Beth. Here's the result, presuming that the bad guys spread their votes evenly:

Bad Guys	Samuel	Alice	John	Theresa	Bob
Number of Votes	500	500	500	500	500

Good Guys	Carol	Ted	Cathy	Maria	Beth
Number of Votes	0	0	750	0	0

See what the good guys did? They cast all their votes for a single nominee, Cathy, and she won the seat over John. There were five directors to be elected, and under cumulative voting shareholders are allowed to cast a number of votes equal to their shareholdings times the number of directorships to be voted upon. Their total votes were 750, 150 × 5. The cumulative voting system thus gives minority shareholders their best chance of obtaining representation on the board of directors. In the example just given it enabled the minority shareholders to win one of the five seats being decided.

DIVIDENDS

Common stockholders have the right to receive *dividends* if the board of directors declares them. Most profitable companies pay out part of their after-tax earnings to shareholders. Dividends are usually paid in cash (cash dividends), but sometimes may be paid in additional shares (stock dividends). It's the board of directors, not the officers, who have absolute authority over the company's dividend policy. They determine if there is going to be any dividend at all, and if there is, they determine the amount and timing of the dividend. They are not legally obligated to pay any dividends on the outstanding common stock even if the company is profitable. Many companies pay out approximately 40% of their after-tax earnings in the form of cash dividends. They reinvest the balance in the business, which effectively shares the profit between the shareholders and the company itself. Companies that are growing very quickly traditionally pay out less in dividends than fully mature businesses, as they need to reinvest almost all their profits to continue to grow the company at a rapid pace. It would make little sense to pay out large dividends if the company had a great need for expansion capital. It is customary for dividend-paying companies to make payments quarterly (four times a year).

CAPITAL GAINS

One reason that investors buy stock is to receive dividends; another reason is the possibility that they may be able to sell their stock for more than they paid for it and thus have a gain. When an investor is able to do this—to buy low and sell high—the profit is known as a *capital gain*. Some investors strive only for income through receiving dividends on stocks or interest on bonds; others are after capital gains; and many investors (possibly *most* investors) are seeking a combination of the two objectives. Generally speaking, more mature investors are primarily interested in income while younger people are more interested in making their capital grow through increases in the prices of their stock investments (capital gains). Income taxes are usually lower on certain capital gains than they are on dividends or interest, making capital gains more attractive for those who are tax-conscious. When a stock is sold after having been held for 12 months or less, the profit or loss is known as a *short-term* gain or loss. For stocks held longer than 12 months, any gain or loss is *long-term*. Long-term gains provide the greatest tax advantages.

PRIMARY AND SECONDARY MARKETS

When stocks are first issued, they are sold by the corporation to investors. The corporation receives the money and the investors receive part ownership in the corporation in the form of shares of common stock. This is known as the *primary* market. After the new shares of stock are all sold by the company, investors are free to sell them to other people. These transactions, in which the corporation is no longer involved, are made in the *secondary* market. If you purchased a new car, a Chevrolet for instance, you bought a newly made item from the manufacturer, General Motors, in exchange for cash. That is a primary market transaction. If, after having owned the car for a year or two, you decide to sell it to a neighbor, that is a secondary market transaction, as General Motors is now out of the picture.

PRICING COMMON STOCKS

Shares of common stock sell for dollars, like most other things in our society. New issues of stock (primary market offerings) generally are priced in the $1 to $50 per share range, while secondary market prices might range from a fraction of $1 to many hundreds (or thousands) of dollars. The securities industry eliminates the dollar sign when showing stock prices, so the price of a stock selling for $1 per share is shown simply as "1"; a $50 per share stock is shown as "50," and so forth. In 2000–2001, the U.S. markets abandoned their long-standing policy of trading stocks in fractions and switched to a decimalized system, thus conforming to the decimal systems used by the other major world financial markets. Some U.S. stocks now trade in increments of $0.05 (nickels), most in increments of $0.01 (pennies).

For nickel increments, the four different per-share prices between $20.00 and $20.25 are: 20.05, 20.10, 20.15, and 20.20.

For penny increments, there are four different per-share prices between $20.00 and $20.05: 20.01, 20.02, 20.03, and 20.04. There are 24 different per-share prices between $20.00 and $20.25.

Pricing Examples

1 share @ 16.35 = $16.35	1 share @ 29.80 = $29.80
10 shares @ 65.30 = $653.00	10 shares @ 44.05 = $440.50
100 shares @ 39.75 = $3,975.00	100 shares @ 8.20 = $820.00
1,000 shares @ 53.00 = $53,000.00	1,000 shares @ 77.75 = $77,750.00

ROUND LOTS AND ODD LOTS

While any number of shares can be purchased, most investors buy them in lots of 100. This is known as a *round lot*, as is any other number of shares divisible by 100, such as 200, 500, 1,300, 4,000 or 55,700. Any number of shares between 1 share and 99 shares is known as an *odd lot*. Quantities of stock such as 16, 51, or 94 shares are all odd lots. It is also possible to buy a mixed lot, such as 138 shares, which consists of a 100-share round lot and an odd lot of 38 shares. The New York Stock Exchange's ticker tape shows only round lot trading; odd lots are counted and reported in the financial press, but they do not show on the tape.

LONG, SHORT, AND FLAT POSITIONS

Security positions are referred to in a unique fashion. If you *own* stock, you are said to be "long" the stock. A long position is positive (+). If you *owe* stock, you are "short" the stock. A short position is negative (−). If you neither own nor owe the stock, you are said to be "flat." A flat position is neutral (0). When discussing positions, each security is accounted for separately; you do not lump all your security positions together. This is a rather important point, especially if you want to be able to carry on a meaningful conversation with a broker. Let's illustrate:

Marianne opens an account with the brokerage firm of Shoreham Brothers. She purchases two different stocks, 100 shares of General Electric and 250 shares of IBM. Marianne pays for the stocks, but instructs her broker to hold the stock certificates at the brokerage firm as she does not want to bother about safeguarding them herself. Every month thereafter, her broker will send her a statement showing her positions as "long 100 General Electric" and "long 250 IBM." Notice that her statement does not say "long 350"; each position is listed separately. Some time later, Marianne tells her broker to sell 60 of her General Electric shares. After the sale, her account will be long 40 GE (the 100 shares she purchased minus the 60 shares she sold) and still long 250 IBM. She then sells all 250 IBM; that reduces her position to long 40 GE, and she is now flat IBM.

Marianne then instructs her broker to send her the remaining shares of GE. Somehow there is an error and Marianne is sent 100 GE even though her position had been reduced to only 40 shares. After the 100 shares are sent to her, Marianne's account will be *short* 60 GE. She owes those "extra" shares to the broker and must return them. After they are returned, her account will be flat with respect to GE. When you own stock you are long; when you owe stock you are short; when you neither own or owe, you are flat.

Long	Short	Flat
Securities *Owned*	Securities *Owed*	Securities Neither
Positive Positions	**Negative** Positions	Owned nor Owed
(+)	(−)	(0)

SUMMARY

All U.S. corporations issue common stock. Common stock is an equity security that normally bears the right to vote, either by the statutory or the cumulative method. Usually purchased for a combination of income (dividends) and growth (capital gains), stocks are considered a high-risk/high-reward investment. Originally offered in the primary (new issue) market, they are subsequently traded in the secondary market, either on a securities exchange (listed) or over-the-counter (unlisted). Round lots are quantities of stock divisible by 100; odd lots are from 1 to 99 shares. The number of shares you own (+) is known as a long position; the number of shares you owe (−) is a short position.

MULTIPLE-CHOICE QUIZ

1. A shareholder owns 150 shares of common stock in a corporation that uses cumulative voting. There are four different directorships to be voted upon. The shareholder wishes to cast as many votes as possible for his favorite choice for one of the seats. How many total votes can he cast for her?

   a. 8

   b. 150

   c. 600

   d. 1,200

2. Dividend-paying corporations traditionally make dividend payments:

   a. twice a month

   b. once a month

   c. quarterly

   d. annually

3. What is the total worth of 100 shares of stock trading at 17.75 per share?

   a. $17.75

   b. $177.50

   c. $1,775.00

   d. $17,750.00

4. Which of the following are considered round lots?

   I   50 shares

   II   100 shares

   III 150 shares

   IV 1,500 shares

   a. II only

   b. I, II, and IV only

   c. II and IV only

   d. I, II, III, and IV

5. Joan Bradley makes her first purchase of Chevron common stock by buying 1,000 shares. Shortly thereafter she buys another 300 shares, and some time later she sells 750 shares. What is her ending position with respect to Chevron shares?

   a. long 550 shares

   b. long 2,050 shares

   c. short 550 shares

   d. short 1,450 shares

PRACTICE EXERCISES

Utilize the following information to answer questions 1 and 2:

The ABC Corporation uses cumulative voting, while the DEF Corporation uses statutory voting.

1. With five directors to be elected, what is the maximum number of votes that a holder of 250 shares of ABC common stock may cast for a single director?

2. With six directors to be elected, what is the maximum number of votes that a holder of 500 shares of DEF common stock may cast for a single director?

3. Thomas Gomez purchases 250 shares of Zenobia Corporation and instructs his broker to hold the shares. The following month Mr. Gomez purchases an additional 400 shares, and the month after that he sells 300 shares. What is his position with respect to shares of Zenobia Corporation after the sale?

Utilize the following information to answer question 4:

A customer's month-end position is as follows:

Long positions	Short positions
100 A	400 M
300 B	800 N
200 C	700 O
500 D	600 P

During the following month, these activities take place:

Purchases	Deliveries	Sales	Receives
500 N	800 L	300 A	200 C
200 B	600 D	100 C	300 Q
400 O	100 R	400 N	900 A
200 A	400 M	900 C	600 P
900 M	300 C	100 P	100 A
200 P	800 R	500 B	200 O

4. What is the customer's ending position? Indicate the number of shares (and whether long, short, or flat) for each position.

MULTIPLE-CHOICE ANSWERS AND EXPLANATIONS

1. **c.** Under cumulative voting, the maximum number of votes is equal to the number of directorships to be decided, multiplied by the number of voting shares owned. These votes may be split among all the candidates in any fashion chosen by the stockholder, and may all be cast for a single director.

2. **c.** Most companies pay dividends quarterly (four times a year). It's not a legal requirement, just custom. The dividend rate may be expressed as so much a quarter or so much a year. A quarterly rate of $1.20 equals an annual rate of $4.80.

3. **c.** Each share is trading at $17.75, so 100 shares are worth $1,775 (100 × 17.75). Answer a is the worth of one share; answer b shows the value of 10 shares; answer d is the value of 1,000 shares. To calculate the total value for 100 shares, simply move the decimal point in the single-share value 2 places to the right. This has the same effect as multiplying by 100.

4. **c.** A round lot is evenly divisible by 100. If the number of shares ends in 2 zeros (00), it's a round lot. Choice I is an odd lot, and choice III is a mixed lot.

5. **a.** After her original purchase of 1,000 shares, Joan was long 1,000. After she bought an additional 300 shares she was long 1,300 (1,000 + 300). After she sold 750 shares her long position was reduced to 550 shares (1,300 − 750). Long positions are created (or increased) by purchases; long positions are eliminated (or reduced) by sales.

ANSWERS TO PRACTICE EXERCISES

1.   1,250 votes

Under cumulative voting, a shareholder's total votes are equal to the number of shares she owns, multiplied by the number of directorships to be voted upon. Her total votes are 1,250 (250 × 5), which may be cast in any manner, including all for a single director.

2.   500 votes

Under statutory voting, shareholders may cast only a number of votes equal to their holdings for any one director. Their holdings are *not* multiplied by the number of directors to be elected, as is the case with cumulative voting.

3.   Long 350 shares

The client purchased 250 shares, which gave him a long (positive) position of 250 shares. The subsequent 400-share purchase added to the position to give him a total long position of 650 shares. The sale of 300 shares reduced the long position by that amount, leaving him with an ending long position of 350 shares. Purchases and receives are positive, sales and deliveries are negative. Get into the habit of referring to any position as long or short—there's a great difference between the two!

4.   Opening long positions are positive (+), as are all purchases and receives. Opening short positions are negative (−), as are all sales and deliveries.

A	long 1,000	+ 100 + 200 − 300 + 900 + 100 = + 1,000
B	flat	+ 300 + 200 − 500 = 0 (flat)
C	short 900	+ 200 − 300 − 100 − 900 + 200 = −900
D	short 100	+ 500 − 600 = − 100
L	short 800	800 delivered from a flat position = − 800
M	long 100	− 400 + 900 − 400 = + 100
N	short 700	− 800 + 500 − 400 = − 700
O	short 100	− 700 + 400 + 200 = − 100
P	long 100	− 600 + 200 − 100 + 600 = + 100
Q	long 300	300 received into a flat position = + 300
R	short 900	900 delivered from a flat position = − 900

Did you remember to include the shares of L, Q, and R? Even though an account might not *begin* a month long or short a given position, there can be activity in that position *during* the month.

CHAPTER 3

Rights and Warrants

RIGHTS

Some corporations specify that their common stockholders are entitled to *preemptive rights*. This means that when the corporation wishes to issue additional shares of common stock, it must first give its current common shareholders the right to buy these additional new shares. This permits current shareholders to maintain their proportionate share of ownership in the corporation. That's quite a statement; here's what it means: If Anita Chirico owns 10 of the 100 shares outstanding of the Treanor Corporation, she owns 10% of the company (10/100 = 10%). If Treanor were now to issue another 100 shares and *not* make them available to Anita, her ownership would be reduced to only 5%, as she would then own only 10 of the 200 shares outstanding (the original 100 shares + the 100 new shares) after the additional issue (10/200 = 5%). This would water down Anita's ownership. Under a preemptive rights arrangement, Mrs. Chirico would be given rights evidencing her ability to buy enough of the new issue to keep her interest in the company at 10%. Since she owns 10% of the old stock, she will receive rights enabling her to buy 10% of the new issue. If she exercises (uses) her rights, she will buy 10 new shares—she is entitled to buy 10% of the new issue—which, together with her original 10-share holding, will give her a total long position of 20 shares, still a 10% ownership position (20/200 = 10%). See how she maintained her proportionate ownership?

If Anita chooses not to exercise her rights (not to invest additional money in Treanor Corporation), she should certainly sell her rights in the open market, because they have value. A rights offering allows investors using the rights to buy stock at a price *under* the stock's current market value. Think of rights as coupons allowing you to buy stock on sale. The coupons (rights) have a value, so if you do not use them you should sell them to someone else. If you do not want to take advantage of the reduced price, other people will, and they will pay you for those "money-saving coupons" known as rights.

The new stock is always issued at a slight discount to the old stock's price, which means the rights to buy at that lower price are worth something. If, for example, the old stock is trading at 48 and you can subscribe to a new share at 45 by using 6 rights, then each right has an approximate value of $0.50. The arithmetic works this way: If you can get new stock at a $3 discount from the price of the currently outstanding stock (48 − 45), and it takes 6 rights to get that discount, then each right will sell for about 1/6 of the $3 discount (3/6 = .5), or $0.50. If the holder of the old shares decides not to subscribe, then he or she should sell the rights to someone else because, after all, they are worth about $0.50 each.

Holders of common stock always receive one right for each share of old stock that they own. If you are long 100 shares, you will receive 100 rights, and if you are long 1,234 shares you will receive 1,234 rights. The number of rights required to subscribe to one new share is determined by the issuing corporation in the following manner: If the company currently has 1,000,000 shares of common stock outstanding and wishes to issue an additional 200,000 shares, the number of rights needed to purchase each new share will be set at 5. Since they must issue one right per outstanding old share, and they have 1,000,000 shares outstanding, they must issue 1,000,000 rights. Since there will be a total of 1,000,000 rights available to buy the 200,000 new shares, it will take 5 rights to purchase each new share (1,000,000 / 200,000 = 5).

MECHANICS OF A RIGHTS OFFERING

Those wishing to subscribe to a rights offering must surrender the appropriate number of rights to the issuing corporation together with the subscription fee. Let's assume that the RQF Corporation is issuing 1,000,000 new common shares under a rights offering. There are 10,000,000 old shares outstanding and they are trading at 97.50 per share. The subscription price for the new shares is 96. If Claudette Morgan owns 200 shares of RQF, she will receive 200 rights. The number of rights needed to subscribe to one new share is 10 (10,000,000 / 1,000,000).

Claudette may either sell her 200 rights for a total of about $30 or buy 20 shares of the new stock by surrendering her 200 rights and subscribing at a cost of $1,920. Here's the arithmetic for each of her choices:

1.   The rights are negotiable instruments, which means they can be sold to another party. Since 10 rights can "save" $1.50 on each new share purchased (97.50 − 96.00), each of the 10 rights should sell for about $0.15

($1.50 / 10). Claudette has 200 rights that should bring in $30 if she sells them (200 × $0.15).

2.   If she chooses to subscribe, Claudette must send her 200 rights to the company together with a payment of $1,920. Her 200 rights can purchase 20 new shares (10 rights for one new share) at the subscription price of $96 per share. That works out to a total cost of $1,920 (20 × $96).

Ms. Morgan can either make $30 on the sale of her rights and still be long 200 shares, or pay out $1,920 (thus exercising her rights) and increase her long position to 220 shares. The choice is hers.

STANDBY UNDERWRITING

In the preceding section we detailed a rights offering of 1,000,000 new shares at 96 per share. The issuing corporation, RQF, hopes to sell these shares for a total of $96,000,000 (1,000,000 × $96), and undoubtedly has earmarked the money for a specific purpose, possibly the construction of a new factory or a similar project. The new shares are attractively priced, 1.50 points below the current market, so selling all the new shares should not be a problem if the price of the old stock stays above the subscription price. But what if the old shares suddenly fall to some price below the subscription price? Then the new shares will no longer be bargain-priced. Investors are not going to buy rights to subscribe at a price *above* the current market, so the rights offering will fail. This is relatively unlikely, but the possibility does exist. To protect itself against this happening, the issuing corporation makes an arrangement with an investment-banking brokerage firm that will guarantee the success of the rights offering. This arrangement is known as a *standby underwriting*. For a fee, usually a few cents per share, the investment banker agrees to buy any unsubscribed shares. Using the figures in our RQF example, this would assure that all 1,000,000 new shares will be bought at $96 per share, and that RQF will get its $96,000,000. RQF does not care who buys the new shares (current shareholders, new investors, or the investment banker), just so long as all the new shares are purchased at the subscription price and RQF gets the money for its project. The issuing corporation is thus guaranteed that its rights offering will raise the full subscription fee, regardless of market conditions.

The investment banker's role actually is quite complicated, but a much simplified explanation goes like this: If the old share price stays above the subscription price, the chances are that many shareholders will subscribe and those who choose not to subscribe will sell their rights to others who, in turn, will subscribe. All the new shares might be bought in this fashion without the investment banker having to do anything except collect its fee. That's a best-case scenario. The downside is that, before anyone has a chance to subscribe, the price of the old stock might plummet to 89. Now there is no reason for anyone to subscribe at 96, and of course no one will. The investment banker will now be forced to buy the 1,000,000 new shares at 96 per share. RQF will get its money and the investment banker will suffer a large loss. Think of the standby underwriting arrangement as a type of insurance. The company buys insurance from the investment banker (the "insurance company") for a premium (the standby fee).

GENERAL CHARACTERISTICS OF RIGHTS

Rights are usually attached to outstanding stock. Rights offerings last for a period of about three weeks, known as the subscription period. Rights have a positive value, at least at the time the offering is announced, because the subscription price is always set below the current market value of the outstanding shares. The secondary market for rights is the same as that for the outstanding shares; if the outstanding shares are listed on a particular stock exchange, the rights (during their brief life) will also trade on that same exchange. Some companies have a preemptive rights provision for their common shares, and some do not.

WARRANTS

Another negotiable instrument that investors can utilize to subscribe for shares is the *warrant*. Warrants work like rights in that they can be surrendered to the issuer, together with the appropriate subscription price, in exchange for new common shares. Warrants differ from rights in a number of ways. They are usually issued as part of a package of new securities rather than being distributed to holders of outstanding securities. Warrants carry a long-term subscription privilege that is usually in the 5- to 10-year range, and sometimes even longer. Warrants do not have a positive value at the time they are issued. In this respect they are similar to deep-out-of-the-money call options. Warrants may trade somewhere other than where the underlying shares trade. The stock can trade on one exchange and its warrants may trade on another exchange or over-the-counter.

A typical warrant might be issued as part of a unit containing another security. Let's trace the history of a hypothetical warrant issued by the Burwell Corporation. Burwell wants to issue bonds but is daunted by the fact that it is going to have to pay 14% interest to the bondholders because, frankly, Burwell's credit rating is not very good. Its bonds will be known as junk bonds, and the investing public demands high interest to compensate them for the risk they take by buying these low-quality instruments that might default. To sweeten the deal, and to lower the interest rate that it will have to pay on the bond issue, Burwell might include a warrant with each new bond and sell the resulting units. Those buying these units get a package deal, one bond and one warrant. The warrant might entitle its owner to buy 100 shares of the company's common stock at $15 per share for the next 10 years. With the warrant attached, Burwell might have to pay only 10% interest on the bond because the warrant gives the unit a speculative appeal.

People might be willing to accept a lower interest rate because they believe that one day they might be able to make money on the warrant. It's like buying a slightly overpriced item because it comes with a lottery ticket! There is a catch, however. At the time the unit is issued, Burwell common stock is selling for 7.75. The warrant's exercise price is 15, well above the current market. It's quite obvious that, under these conditions, the warrant has absolutely no value at the present time. It makes no sense to surrender a warrant, and $1,500, to receive 100 shares of stock worth $775. Then why the appeal? People reason that, given such a long time period (10 years), the stock may very well trade much higher than 15 while the warrant is still "alive."

If and when the stock does trade higher than the warrant's exercise price of 15, *then* the warrant will have a positive value. For example, if the stock sold up to 24, then the warrant would be worth a minimum of $900. Purchasing 100 shares of stock in the open market at 24 would cost $2,400, but using the warrant to purchase 100 shares at 15 would cost only $1,500, a saving of $900. The warrant, originally issued as an out-of-the-money instrument, would now be in-the-money.

SUMMARY

Rights and warrants are *common stock equivalents* in that their exercise will cause more common stock to be outstanding. Convertible preferred stock and convertible bonds are also common stock equivalents. While rights are short-term options, warrants are long-term instruments. At issuance, rights have a positive value while warrants have a negative value. Holders of rights and warrants do not vote, nor do they receive dividends. Those owning rights or warrants have the ability to buy stock at a specified price (the exercise price) until the expiration date. Rights and warrants are transferable and can be traded in the open market. Rights are usually attached to existing issues; warrants are generally issued in connection with a new issue as a sweetener to make the new issue more attractive.

MULTIPLE-CHOICE QUIZ

Answer questions 1 to 4 using the following information:

An investor owns 1,000 shares of XYZ, and XYZ announces a rights offering. There are 25,000,000 shares outstanding and the company is offering an additional 2,500,000 shares at 36 per share. The market price of the outstanding stock is 37.25.

1. How many rights will the shareholder receive?
    a. 10
    b. 25
    c. 100
    d. 1,000

2. How many new shares is the investor entitled to subscribe for?
    a. 10
    b. 25
    c. 100
    d. 1,000

3. If the investor chooses to subscribe, what will the total subscription cost be?
    a. $3,600
    b. $3,725
    c. $36,000
    d. $37,250

4. If the investor chooses not to subscribe and instead sells the rights, approximately how much will the investor receive?
    a. $1.25
    b. $12.50
    c. $125.00
    d. $1,250.00

5. Which of the following are common stock equivalents?
    I   straight preferred stocks
    II   convertible preferred stocks
    III rights
    IV   warrants
    a. II only
    b. III and IV only
    c. II, III, and IV only
    d. I, II, III, and IV

PRACTICE EXERCISES

The Gneiding Corporation is going to offer 500,000 shares of additional common stock through a rights offering. The company presently has 5,000,000 common shares outstanding. The per-share subscription price for the new shares will be $68.00. Ms. Theresa Manley currently owns 100 shares of the outstanding stock.

1.   How many subscription rights will Theresa receive?

2.   How many new shares will she be entitled to subscribe for?

3.   Presuming she chooses to subscribe, how much additional money must Ms. Manley invest?

4.   If she chooses *not* to subscribe for the new shares but simply to retain the shares she already owns, what is her best course of action?

MULTIPLE-CHOICE ANSWERS AND EXPLANATIONS

1. **d.** Shareholders always receive one right per "old" share owned. Do not confuse the number of rights received with the number of rights needed to subscribe.

2. **c.** Since there are a total of 25,000,000 shares outstanding and the company plans to issue an additional 2,500,000 shares, it will require 10 rights to subscribe for one new share (25,000,000 / 2,500,000 = 10). It's called a one-for-ten deal, meaning that you can subscribe for one new share for every ten old shares you own. The investor who owns 1,000 shares will be entitled to subscribe for one-tenth as many new shares, or 100 shares of new stock.

3. **a.** The investor is entitled to subscribe for 100 new shares at a subscription price of $36 per share (100 x $36 = $3,600).

4. **c.** Ten rights enable you to buy one new share at 36 rather than 37.25. Thus, 10 rights afford a saving of $1.25 (37.25 − 36). Each right is therefore worth $0.125 ($1.25/10). The rights would trade for about $0.125 each. The 1,000 rights received would bring in $125.00 (1,000 × $0.125).

5. **c.** The only security listed that is not a common stock equivalent is the straight (nonconvertible) preferred stock. Convertible bonds are also common stock equivalents. Common stock equivalents can cause the issuance of additional common shares.

ANSWERS TO PRACTICE EXERCISES

1. She will receive 100 subscription rights.

   An investor always receives one right per old (outstanding) share held.

2. She is entitled to subscribe for 10 new shares.

   Since there are 5,000,000 old shares outstanding and the company is going to issue only 500,000 new shares (one-tenth as many as are currently outstanding), investors are entitled to subscribe for one-tenth the number of shares they currently own. The client owns 100 shares and may subscribe for one-tenth that number of new shares ($1/10 \times 100$), or 10 additional shares.

3. $680

   Ten new shares (see answer 2) at $68.00 per share will cost a total of $680.

4. She should sell the rights.

   Investors who choose not to use their rights are best advised to sell them. The rights have value and should not be ignored—either subscribe to the additional shares or sell the rights.

CHAPTER 4

Preferred Stock

The only type of security that a corporation *must* issue is common stock, an equity (ownership) security. Corporations *may* choose to issue another type of equity security known as *preferred* stock. Preferred stock differs from common stock in a number of ways.

FIXED DIVIDENDS

The dividend rate on common stock may fluctuate. It would be relatively rare (and disappointing to most shareholders) for a common stock to pay the same dividend year in and year out. Many investors buy common stocks because they anticipate that the dividend will be increased over time. During good times the board of directors may choose to pay the common stockholders a one-time extra dividend, or they might increase the quarterly rate. That's like getting a raise! On the other hand, if poor business conditions prevail, the board of directors might reduce the common stock dividend or even eliminate it altogether.

Preferred stocks have a *fixed* dividend rate. In this respect they are very similar to bonds. Bonds and preferred stocks are collectively referred to as fixed-income securities. A preferred stock's fixed dividend rate is announced at the time the stock is first offered and does not change over time. (There are variable-rate preferreds and participating preferreds that have changeable dividends, but they are beyond the scope of this book.) This fixed, predictable stream of dividends is very comforting to investors who are interested primarily in income, because they know in advance precisely what their income will be. The fixed rate is both the good news and the bad news. The dividend on a preferred stock does not go down when business falters, but it does not go up when business is booming. A very broad rule of thumb is that more conservative investors gravitate toward preferred stock while more adventurous people are willing to assume the larger risks (and larger potential rewards) of investing in common stocks. Many investors, both individuals and institutions, invest in both types of equity security.

MULTIPLE CLASSES OF STOCK

Corporations usually have only a single class of common stock outstanding, but most companies that issue preferred stock eventually issue several different classes of these fixed-dividend securities. If we wish to refer to XYZ common stock, we have only to write or say "XYZ common," or even simply "XYZ," and everyone will understand that we mean XYZ's single class of common stock. If, as is probable, XYZ has issued several different classes of preferred stock, it will be insufficient to say "XYZ preferred" because there will be confusion about which particular issue of preferred we are referring to. The different classes of preferred stock issued by a corporation are distinguished, one from another, by adding some identifying information to the security's name, as in these examples:

1.   XYZ $4.00 preferred, XYZ $6.00 preferred

2.   XYZ 7% preferred, XYZ 9% preferred

3.   XYZ A preferred, XYZ B preferred

In example 1, we differentiated between the two issues by showing dollar amounts ($4.00 and $6.00) that represent the amount of each preferred's annual dividend. Since dividends are paid on a quarterly basis, each quarter's dividend will be one-fourth the annual rate. The $4.00 preferred will pay $1.00 per quarter ($4.00 per year) and the $6.00 preferred will pay $1.50 per quarter ($6.00 per year).

In example 2, each issue shows a different percentage rate (7% and 9%) rather than a dollar amount. This reveals the annual dividend in a different way—it indicates the particular percentage of that preferred's par value that will be paid as a cash dividend each year. (Par value is explained in detail in the following section.) Assuming that both preferred stocks had $100 par value, then the 7% preferred would have an annual dividend rate of $7.00 (7% of $100), which works out to a quarterly rate of $1.75 per share. The 9% preferred would have an annual dividend of $9.00 (9% of $100), and a quarterly rate of $2.25. If the par value of the 7% preferred happened to be $50, then its annual dividend would be just $3.50 (7% of $50).

Some companies, particularly those with a number of different preferred issues outstanding, use the alphabet system and simply name them "A," "B," "C," and so forth, as in example 3. In this latter system there is no way of determining the preferred stock's dividend rate simply from its name.

PAR VALUE

Both common and preferred stocks have an assigned par value. For common stocks it might be a dollars-and-cents value such as $0.10, or $1.00, or $15.00; sometimes a common stock is said to be "no par." The par value (if any) of a common stock has no relationship to its original price at issuance, its dividend, or its current market value; it's simply a bookkeeping item of interest only to the company's accountants. A common stock's par value is not taken into account when it is being evaluated as a possible investment. The par value of preferred shares, on the other hand, is quite important and is utilized in a number of ways by investors and security analysts.

Preferred shares are usually issued at, or very close to, their assigned par values. A $100 par preferred stock was probably issued at just about $100 per share. While $100 is a very common par value for preferred stocks, it is certainly not the only one. If a stock is described as a 10% preferred, you have no way of telling from that information alone the exact amount of the annual dividend. The dividend is 10% of the stock's par value. If the par value happens to be $50, then the annual dividend rate is $5 (10% of $50); if the stock's par value is $100, then the annual dividend is $10 (10% of $100).

SENIORITY OF PREFERRED DIVIDENDS

A preferred stock is senior to common stock in several respects. The dividends on all the preferred issues of a given company must be paid, in full, before any dividends at all may be paid to the common stockholders. This is comforting to the owners of preferred stock—they know that their dividends come first. In this respect, preferred stocks are safer than common shares of the same company. Preferred stocks do not have the same growth potential as common stocks, but they are less risky. All preferred stocks are not necessarily safe, and all common stocks are not necessarily risky. The common stock of company A might be a much better investment than the preferred stock of company B. Each issue must be judged on its own merits. Generally speaking, more conservative investors, those interested primarily in the receipt of fairly dependable income, are more interested in preferred stocks than are investors who are seeking growth and are willing to assume the risks involved. In most instances, preferred stocks are bought for income and common stocks are bought for income and capital gain.

CUMULATIVE PREFERRED

Virtually all preferred issues are *cumulative*, meaning that if the directors are ever forced to skip one or more preferred dividends (because of extremely poor cash-flow conditions), those passed-over dividends are still owed to the preferred shareholders and must eventually be paid. Note that the word *cumulative* has several different meanings with respect to securities. We distinguished between cumulative and statutory voting in Chapter 2, and the same word also describes how arrears on most preferred issues are treated. For example, the A. Sund Corporation has an issue of $8 preferred outstanding and is unable to pay the first quarterly dividend of $2. This becomes an arrearage and the amount is still due to the preferred shareholders. If the company skips the next quarterly dividend as well, the arrearage becomes $4. When the company recovers from its cash problems, the arrearages will be paid. While there are any arrearages on preferred stock, that company's common stockholders may not receive any dividends at all. All back dividends on that company's preferred stock must be paid up before dividends to the common stockholders may resume. This is another example of the seniority of preferred stock.

PREFERRED STOCKHOLDERS' RIGHTS WHEN A COMPANY IS DISSOLVED

Preferred stock is senior to common stock in still another respect. When a company is dissolved, either voluntarily or involuntarily (bankruptcy), the first stockholders to be repaid are the owners of preferred stock. Presuming there is any money left by the time it is the preferred shareholders' turn to be paid off, they are entitled to receive par value for their shares. The holders of $50 par preferred receive $50 per share, $100 par preferred shareholders receive $100 per share, and so on. That's another reason that investors should be aware of the par value of their preferred stocks: It indicates the per-share amount of their claim if and when the company is dissolved. Common stockholders receive whatever may be left after everyone else has been paid. Employees and the taxing authorities are the first in line, then the creditors (including bondholders), then preferred shareholders, and finally the common stockholders. Most of the time there isn't any money left when the time comes to deal with the common stockholders, and sometimes even the bondholders and preferred shareholders receive nothing or only a partial payment.

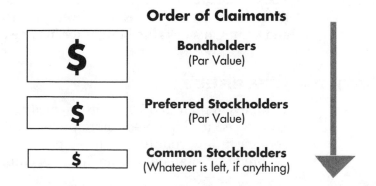

Order of Claimants

Bondholders
(Par Value)

Preferred Stockholders
(Par Value)

Common Stockholders
(Whatever is left, if anything)

VOTING

Most common stock votes, but most preferred stock does not vote. Some companies have a special rule that gradually shifts the vote from the common to the preferred shareholders if there are arrears on the preferred dividends, but that's relatively rare. Even though it usually does not vote, preferred stock is still considered an equity (ownership) security like common stock.

SIMILARITY TO BONDS

Preferred stocks are very similar to bonds. Both have fixed cash payments (fixed dividends for preferreds and fixed interest for bonds); both have seniority over common stocks with respect to cash distributions (bonds first); both have priority of claim in dissolution (again, bonds first); and neither type of security usually votes. Bonds and preferred stocks are sometimes referred to as fixed-income securities. Most large *portfolios* (collections of securities) contain a mix of common stocks, preferred stocks, and bonds. These portfolios contain a greater proportion of fixed-income securities when the objective is income and relative safety, and more common stocks when the objective is growth. Juggling the mix among the various types of investments is known as *asset allocation*.

CALLABLE PREFERRED

Some preferred issues are *callable*. This means that the corporation has the right to redeem the stock for cash. Once preferred stock is called, it ceases to pay dividends and must be turned in. The call price (the amount of money received by the stockholders for each share of called preferred) is the stock's par value, and sometimes a small premium as well. The call feature is beneficial to the issuing company, not to the shareowners. Many preferred issues are called when current interest rates are substantially lower than they were at the time the callable preferred was first issued. If a company has issued a 15% callable preferred and several years later finds that it can now issue another preferred stock with a much lower dividend rate, say 8%, it will issue a new class of preferred stock and use the proceeds to retire the earlier issue by calling it. It will thus be refinancing its preferred stocks by issuing an 8% preferred and retiring a 15% preferred, saving a great deal of money. Now the shareholders who were called are forced to reinvest their cash at a time when interest rates are fairly low. In effect, a preferred issue is likely to be called just when stockholders least want it to be called—they are happy to have a high-yield investment in a low-yield environment, and then the issuer takes it away.

A typical callable preferred might work something like this: In 2003, RQF Corporation wishes to issue a new class of $100 par preferred at a price of $100 per share. The company wants the stock to be callable, but appreciates that this might make the new issue unattractive to the investing public. It might compromise by guaranteeing that the issue won't be called for the first five years after issuance, but would then be callable at $105 (a 5% premium) beginning in the year 2008, at $103 beginning in 2010, at $101 in 2012, and at par ($100) in 2014 and later. This call feature on RQF preferred might be described as "five-year call protection, initially callable at a 5% premium, scaled down to par in 2014." That's the way the stock brokerage community would report it. Many bonds are also callable; the principle is the same.

INTEREST-RATE SENSITIVITY

Fixed-income securities, such as preferred stocks, are said to be *interest-rate sensitive*. When interest rates rise, the prices of preferred stocks tend to go down. When interest rates decline, preferred share prices go up. Interest rates and preferred share prices are said to be inversely proportional.

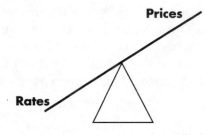

Here's an example: Marobeth Corporation issued a 12% preferred ($100 par) in 1995. Then-current interest rates called for a 12% return on preferred issues of that quality, as money was tight and the returns on other investments at that time were equally high. Marobeth was forced to pay 12%, because that was the rate then demanded by the investing public and it was possible for Marobeth to float a new preferred issue only at competitive rates. Each share of the 12% preferred paid $12 annually (12% of $100).

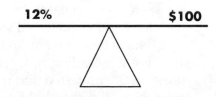

By 2000, interest rates had fallen dramatically and new issues of $100 par preferred shares of comparable quality were being sold at 9% and were paying an annual dividend of only $9 (9% of $100). The 12% preferred had become a very desirable investment because it was paying substantially more than new issues. At least in theory, the 12% preferred would be so much in demand that people would pay substantially more than par for it, even bidding up its price so high that its yield will fall to the "new" rate of 9%. Here's the arithmetic: When the preferred was first issued, its current yield was 12% ($12/$100). The new preferreds are yielding 9% ($9/$100). Investors will be attracted to the old issue because it pays substantially higher dividends. The market will eventually stabilize when the older preferred is trading at about $133 per share, the price at which its current yield would also be 9% ($12/$133).

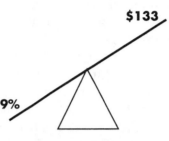

Let's explore what would have happened to the price of our 12% preferred if interest rates had *risen* substantially after it had been issued. If rates had gone up to 15%, our 12% issue could no longer compete and would fall out of favor. Its price would decline to approximately $80, where it would be yielding the "new" rate of 15% ($12/$80 = 15%). That's the way the fixed-income market works—as interest rates change, prices change too, so that yields are adjusted to current interest levels. The subject of yields is discussed thoroughly in a later chapter, as it is quite important to investors.

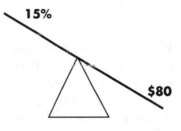

CONVERTIBLE PREFERRED

Some preferred issues are *convertible*. This means that the preferred shareholder has the option of exchanging the stock for another security, usually common stock of the same corporation. Note that the *company* has the right to call an issue (if it's callable), but the *shareholder* has the right to convert an issue (if it's convertible).

Convertible preferreds seem to give the investor the best of all worlds: They are senior securities with dividends that must be paid in full before any dividends may be paid on the common stock; they have seniority over common stock if the company is dissolved; and they offer a chance for capital gains as well. They are considered safer than common stocks but, being convertible into common stock, they also offer the prospect of dramatic capital gains if the company does very well.

Straight (nonconvertible) preferreds usually offer only stability of income and relative safety, but not growth. With a convertible issue, the growth possibility is there as well. As always, there is a price for this additional feature: Convertible preferreds usually have a lower dividend rate than straight preferreds of similar quality. An investor who wants a preferred stock with a growth "kicker" must be willing to accept a lower return while holding the preferred, hoping that over time the common stock will rise greatly in price and the investor can then switch (convert) to the common stock.

The number of shares of common stock that will be received upon conversion of a share of convertible preferred stock is known as its *conversion ratio*. If a share of XYZ cvt. pfd. (convertible preferred) may be exchanged for 5 shares of XYZ common stock, it is said to have a conversion ratio of 5.

Sometimes financial publications will indicate instead the convertible preferred's *conversion price*. The conversion price can be changed into the conversion ratio by dividing it into the preferred's par value. For instance, if a $100 par convertible preferred has a conversion price of 50 (sometimes shown as $50), you simply divide the par value by the conversion price to arrive at the conversion ratio: $100 / 50 = 2. In this example the conversion *price* of 50 works out to a conversion *ratio* of 2.

Most individual investors can better appreciate the concept of the conversion ratio (How many shares of common will I receive?), rather than the conversion price that is most often used by financial industry professionals.

PARITY

When market prices of a convertible security and its underlying common stock are in balance, they are said to be *at parity*. If a preferred stock trading at 120 is exchangeable for 5 shares of common stock, and that common stock has a current market value of 24.00, they are in balance ($120 = 5 \times 24.00$). A preferred stock exchangeable for 10 shares of common stock trading at 14.50 would be at parity if it were trading at 145 ($10 \times 14.50 = 145$).

SUMMARY

Although they are equity securities, preferred stocks have many of the features of bonds. Most preferred issues do not carry the right to vote. They offer a fixed dividend and, in general, are considered safer than common stocks. The vast majority of preferred issues are cumulative, and shareholders are entitled to receive their par value if and when the company is liquidated. Both their rights to dividends and their rights in liquidation are senior to those of holders of common stock. Some preferred issues are callable, some are convertible, and some have both of these features.

Preferred stock prices are sensitive to changes in interest rates and are inversely proportional to them. These senior securities are usually purchased by relatively conservative investors for their predictable income.

MULTIPLE-CHOICE QUIZ

1. Which of the following are considered to be fixed-income securities?

    I   common stocks

    II straight preferred stocks

    III convertible preferred stocks

    IV bonds

    a. I and II only

    b. II and III only

    c. III and IV only

    d. II, III, and IV only

2. An 8% preferred stock with a $25 par value will pay a quarterly dividend of:

    a. $0.50

    b. $1.00

    c. $2.00

    d. $8.00

3. Arrange the following in the order that they will be paid off in the event a company is liquidated.

    I   preferred stockholders

    II employees

    III common stockholders

    IV bondholders

    a. IV, II, III, I

    b. I, III, IV, II

    c. II, IV, I, III

    d. III, I, II, IV

4. Callable preferred issues would most likely be called during times of:

    a. good business

    b. poor business

    c. increasing interest rates

    d. decreasing interest rates

5. NFW convertible preferred ($100 par) has a conversion price of 25. How many shares of common will be received for each share of preferred converted?

    a. .25

    b. 2.5

    c. 4

    d. 25

PRACTICE EXERCISES

An investor is considering the purchase of 100 shares of Cartlidge Company 9% convertible preferred stock, $100 par. The conversion price is 25.00

1. What is the dollar amount of the *quarterly* dividend the customer might expect?

2. If the client purchases the preferred stock and converts at a later date, what will he receive in exchange?

3. How might the yield on this preferred stock compare with the yield on another company's straight (nonconvertible) preferred of the same quality?

4. What is the preferred issue's relative safety compared with the same company's bonds and common stock?

MULTIPLE-CHOICE ANSWERS AND EXPLANATIONS

1. **d.** Bonds and preferred issues, whether convertible or straight, are considered fixed-income investments. There are some preferred issues and bonds that may have a variable rate (or even no rate at all, such as zero-coupon bonds), but these certainly are the exception rather than the rule.

2. **a.** The stock pays 8% of its par value annually; 8% of $25 is $2.00 (the annual dividend), which works out to a quarterly rate of $0.50.

3. **c.** Employees and the tax authorities always come first. When it's the investors' turn, the bondholders are first, then the preferred shareholders, and last the common shareholders. In the unlikely event that there is more than enough money to satisfy everyone, then the common shareholders receive the balance.

4. **d.** Companies are more likely to refinance their outstanding securities when interest rates are falling. This means it will be cheaper for them to borrow funds by issuing bonds, or to sell new preferred issues at lower rates, in order to retire other issues that pay higher dividends or interest.

5. **c.** You can determine a convertible security's conversion ratio by dividing its par value by the conversion price: $100 / 25 = 4$. The mathematics are precisely the same for convertible bonds although, as we shall learn, we consider all bonds to have a par value of $1,000.

ANSWERS TO PRACTICE EXERCISES

1. His quarterly dividend will be $225 ($2.25 per share).

    A 9% preferred stock ($100 par) pays $9.00 per share annually (9% × $100). Each *quarterly* dividend will be for one-fourth of that amount.

2. Four shares of Cartlidge Company common stock for each preferred share exchanged, for a total of 400 shares of common if all 100 shares of preferred were exchanged.

    A $100 par preferred stock with a conversion *price* of 25.00 has a conversion *ratio* of 4 (100 / 25.00 = 4).

3. The yield on this convertible preferred stock will be lower.

    That's the "cost" to the purchaser of a convertible preferred stock; the investor must accept a lower yield than that to be expected from a straight (nonconvertible) preferred of similar quality.

4. The preferred stock is less secure than the company's bonds, but more secure than the company's common stock.

    Within a given company, that's the order of security—bonds first, then preferred, and common stock last.

CHAPTER 5

Dividends

Dividends are usually paid in cash, but sometimes are paid in stock (stock dividends). It is traditional that dividend-paying corporations distribute their dividends four times a year. Most companies strive to maintain a given dividend rate once it is established, and to raise it over time, but this is impossible for companies (such as automobile manufacturers) in cyclical industries. The *dividend payout ratio* shows the percentage of the company's net earnings that are paid out as dividends to the common stockholders. If the Adelphi Corporation had earnings per share of $1.20 and paid an annual dividend of $0.40 per share on its common stock, the dividend payout ratio would be 33% ($0.40 / $1.20 = 33%). Companies in mature industries, such as utilities, tend to have high payout ratios, and fast-growing businesses tend to pay out less in favor of retaining more of their earnings to plow back into the companies to finance rapid expansion.

REGULAR-WAY SETTLEMENT

To better understand the timing of dividend payments, it is necessary to know about trade settlement. When you buy or sell a stock through a brokerage firm, you will receive a *confirmation* shortly after the transaction is completed. Also known simply as a "confirm," this document lists the details of the trade such as your name and account number, the number of shares involved, the price per share, the commission charged, and other relevant data. Ordinarily your stockbroker (account executive, registered representative, or financial consultant) will have telephoned you with a verbal report before you receive the confirm in the mail; the confirm is the formal written notification. It shows "final money," which is the amount you owe on a purchase or the amount due you on a sale. There are two dates on the confirm, the *trade date* and the *settlement date*.

The trade date is simply the day the actual purchase or sale took place, either on a stock exchange or over-the-counter. The settlement date indicates the deadline for your payment if you have purchased something, or the date on which the broker can pay you for securities that you have sold. The settlement date for almost all stock transactions (and corporate and municipal bond transactions as well) is three business days after the trade date. This is known as "T + 3." If you buy or sell a stock on Monday, January 8, the trade will settle on Thursday, January 11. That's three *business* days after the trade date. If there are no holidays during the three business days following a trade, *regular-way* settlement (T + 3) trades settle like this: Monday's trades settle on Thursday of the same week, Tuesday's trades settle on Friday of that week, Wednesday's trades settle the following Monday, Thursday's trades settle the following Tuesday, and Friday's trades settle the following Wednesday. If any of the three weekdays following the trade is a holiday, then the settlement is delayed another day.

The settlement date is important for a number of reasons. It is the due date for payments to and from a broker; it is the date that the trade is "posted" to the customer's monthly statement; and it is the date that a buying customer's name is officially entered on the transfer agent's record books as the owner of the stock. Let's take these points one at a time. We will use the same trade information in each of our examples.

Diane Flood calls her broker on Wednesday, October 19, and enters an order to buy 100 General Motors. The order is executed that same day. Mrs. Flood will receive a confirm relating to this purchase that will show the price per share that she paid, the commission she was charged, the final money due (the total amount), the trade date of October 19, and the settlement date of October 24, the following Monday. Mrs. Flood is supposed to pay for her stock by the settlement date, October 24, at the latest (presuming she does not have a sufficient credit balance in her brokerage account). That helps to explain why the settlement date is sometimes referred to as the "due" date—it's when the customer's money is due. Even though Diane does not make payment until the 24th, she is still considered to be an owner of the stock, and has been since the trade was actually executed, probably just minutes after she entered her buy order on October 19.

Mrs. Flood's trade will be posted on her October monthly statement under the date of October 24, the settlement date. She bought the stock on the 19th, and has owned the stock since the 19th, but her monthly statement shows her buy trade as of the 24th. In fact, had Mrs. Flood bought her stock later in the month, say on October 29 or 30, the trade would not show on her October statement at all, but would be posted on her November statement on a settlement date early in that month, which is when a late-October trade would settle. We say that "trades are posted to the monthly statement according to settlement date." It is not until October 24, the settlement date, that GM's transfer agent will officially list Mrs. Flood as a stockholder. It takes three business days. She has owned the stock since the 19th, but she is not "listed" as an owner until the 24th. Remember that it is the transfer agent that keeps track of the people who own the stock, and the transfer agent that normally distributes the cash dividends. It makes sense that the organization that is supposed to know who owns the stock is also charged with the responsibility for distributing dividends.

Regular-way settlement for stocks, corporate bonds, and municipal bonds is three business days (T + 3). Regular-way settlement for options and government bonds is the next business day (T + 1). There are other arrangements for settlement beside regular-way, including cash (same-day), next-day, and seller's option, but these are used only rarely.

	T+3	T+1
Products	Stocks, corporate and municipal bonds	Options and government bonds
Purchase Date	Wednesday Oct. 19	Wednesday Oct. 19
Settlement Date	Monday Oct. 24	Thursday Oct. 20

THE MECHANICS OF A CASH DIVIDEND DISTRIBUTION

A company's board of directors usually meets to decide dividend policy four times a year. Assuming they decide that a cash dividend will be paid, an announcement is made to the financial press. The day the news is disclosed is known as the *declaration date*. The company announces the amount of the dividend, the *record date*, and the *payment date*. Soon thereafter, a fourth date, the *ex-dividend date*, is set by either a stock exchange or the NASD (National Association of Securities Dealers). This date, the "ex" date, falls between the declaration date and the record date. The four dates, in chronological order, are the declaration date, the ex-dividend date, the record date, and the payment date.

The declaration date is simply the date when the dividend announcement is made public. It is usually the same day that the board met but, in theory, they could meet for dividend action on a given day and not make the announcement until a later date. The details about the dividend, including the per-share amount, the record date, and the payment date, will be printed in the financial press. Popular sources for such information include the *Wall Street Journal* and *Standard & Poor's Dividend Record*.

The ex-dividend date is not set by the corporation. It is set by the stock exchange on which the shares are traded if the stock is listed, by the NASD for over-the-counter stocks, and for mutual funds, by the funds themselves. The ex-dividend date is the first trading day that the stock trades *without* the dividend. If you are interested in receiving a forthcoming dividend, you must purchase the stock *before* the ex-dividend date (or "cum" dividend). If you buy the stock on or after the ex date, you will *not* receive the dividend. The ex date is usually set two business days before the record date.

The record date is for the use of the dividend disbursing agent. Whoever is listed as a shareholder on the transfer agent's books at the close of business on the record date will receive the dividend. That's the deciding factor as to who gets the dividend; if you are listed as a shareholder at the close of business on the record date, then you will receive the dividend. The payment date is the date that the shareholders will actually receive their dividend payments.

XYZ Corporation (listed on a stock exchange) declares a $1.00 per share dividend on its common stock. The timetable might look like this:

	Date	Set By
Declaration Date	January 10	XYZ
Ex-Dividend Date	January 23	Exchange
Record Date	January 25	XYZ
Payment Date	February 9	XYZ

The declaration date, the record date, and the payment date were all set by XYZ; the ex date was set by the stock exchange.

Here's a portion of the calendar for that January:

Sun	Mon	Tue	Wed	Thu	Fri	Sat
13	14	15	16	17	18	19
20	21	22	**23 (ex)**	24	**25 (rec)**	26
27	28	29	30	31		

Here's how the ex date, the record date, and regular-way settlement all tie together: Since the ex date is January 23, XYZ stock must be purchased before that date to receive the dividend. It follows that the last day to buy the stock so as to receive the dividend will be the business day just before the ex date. That "last chance to buy the stock and receive the dividend" day is Tuesday, January 22, the last business day before the ex date. If XYZ is purchased on January 22, the purchaser will be listed on the shareholder lists three business days later, on January 25. That's the record date, three business days after the trade date. So a January 22 buyer just makes it, being listed as a shareholder on the record date and therefore entitled to receive the dividend. Think of the ex date as a notice to buyers that the dividend is now gone—that buyers of the stock on and after the ex date are not entitled to the dividend. "Ex" means without the dividend.

An investor who waited until January 23 (the ex date) to buy the stock would be listed as a shareholder by the transfer agent three business days later, on Monday, January 28. Since the record date was the previous Friday, January 25, that investor is not entitled to receive the dividend. Those who purchase the stock before the ex-dividend date are entitled to the dividend; those who purchase the stock on or after the ex-dividend date are not.

PRICE CHANGES ON THE EX-DIVIDEND DATE

There should be no need for investors to be in a hurry to buy a stock before its ex-dividend date so as not to miss out on the next cash dividend. You do not lose if you miss out on the dividend, because the stock will probably decline in price on the ex-dividend date by the approximate amount of the dividend. What you miss in dividends you will make up for in price. If a stock is selling at 60, cum dividend, it will probably decline to about 59 on the day that it goes "ex" for a $1 per share cash dividend. If you pay 60 you will receive a share of stock and a $1 dividend; if you pay 59 you will receive only a share of stock. Actually, you are better off not receiving that particular dividend! Why pay an extra dollar to receive that same dollar back almost immediately as a dividend that is taxable?

If a stock closes at 48.50 on a given day, and then trades "ex" a $0.50 dividend the following day, it is considered to be *unchanged* in price from day to day if it closes at 48.00 on the ex-dividend day. A stock priced at 48.50 with a soon-to-be-paid dividend of $0.50 did not actually decrease in value if it next traded at 48.00 *without* the $0.50 dividend. If that same stock closed at 48.10 on the ex-dividend day, the financial press would report that the stock was *up* $0.10, not *off* $0.40. The previous day's closing price must be adjusted for the amount of the dividend so that the cum-dividend value can be properly compared with the ex-dividend value.

STOCK DIVIDENDS

Occasionally a corporation will pay a *stock dividend* in addition to (or instead of) a cash dividend. The amount of the stock dividend is expressed as a percentage such as 10% or 25%. If you own 200 shares of DEF and it pays a 10% stock dividend, you will receive an additional 20 shares of stock (10% × 200 = 20) and will then own a total of 220 shares. Your proportionate share of ownership in the corporation is unchanged because everyone gets the same 10% stock dividend. You now own 10% more shares than before the stock dividend, but so does everyone else, so your ownership interest did not increase. Corporations pay stock dividends for several reasons: Investors like to receive them, and they save the company money in that they are able to issue additional shares rather than paying cash. At least in theory, the per-share price of the stock declines after a stock dividend. If your 200 shares were worth $13,000 before you received the stock dividend (they were trading at 65), then the 220 shares owned after the stock dividend should be worth the same amount. Your 220 shares are still worth just about $13,000, so each of them is now worth about $59 ($13,000 / 220). A stock dividend does not necessarily make you richer; you simply become the owner of more shares. The fact that the shares will trade at a lower price after the stock dividend might be considered good news because, for some strange reason, lower-priced shares are more attractive to individual investors.

Stock Splits

Many companies *split* their shares, especially when they trade at relatively high prices such as 70, 80, or 90 per share. Again, as with stock dividends, you do not own anything more after the split than before the split, just a greater number of shares. The most common split is 2-for-1, actually very similar to a 100% stock dividend. If you own 100 shares before a 2-for-1 split, you will receive another 100 shares and will then own a total of 200 shares. In theory, the stock will sell after the split at about one-half its per-share value before the split. If the stock had been selling at 86 before the split, it will sell for approximately 43 after the split. Since individuals are more likely to buy relatively low-priced stocks rather than higher-priced stocks, splitting an issue (and consequently lowering its price) makes it more attractive to the investing public.

Dividend Reinvestment Plans

Some publicly held corporations make a *dividend reinvestment* plan available to their shareholders. Under such a plan, shareholders may automatically reinvest their cash dividends in additional shares of the company's stock. This is similar to compounding your interest in a bank account. Many companies encourage the practice by absorbing some or all of the commission charges on the reinvestments, or even making the additional shares available at a discount. It is important for shareholders to realize that reinvested dividends are taxable.

Current Yield

The percentage return on a dividend-paying stock is sometimes expressed as its current yield. It is found by dividing a stock's annual dividend by its current price per share. Example: GHI pays an annual dividend of $1.60 ($0.40 per quarter) and is trading at 31.35. Its current yield is 5.1% ($1.60 / 31.35). The calculation of current yield does not take into account changes in the stock's price; a much more sophisticated calculation known as total return measures dividend income as well as capital appreciation or depreciation.

SUMMARY

Regular-way settlement for stocks, corporate bonds, and municipal bonds is three business days after the trade date (T + 3). Dividends may be paid in cash or stock. The amount of the dividend, if any, is set by the board of directors. The board establishes the declaration, record, and payment dates; the stock exchange or the NASD sets the ex-dividend date. The ex-dividend date for a cash distribution is usually set two business days prior to the record date. To be entitled to a cash dividend, an investor must purchase the stock prior to the ex-dividend date. Doing so causes the investor's name to be entered into the transfer agent's books by the record date. Stocks decline in price on the ex-dividend date by approximately the amount of the dividend. Current yield is calculated by dividing a stock's annual dividend by its current price.

MULTIPLE-CHOICE QUIZ

1. A corporation has set the record date for its next cash dividend as Wednesday, August 12. What ex-dividend date will be set for this distribution?

    a. Wednesday, August 5

    b. Thursday, August 6

    c. Friday, August 7

    d. Monday, August 10

2. The amount of a company's dividend is set by the:

    a. shareholders

    b. NASD

    c. corporate officers

    d. board of directors

3. What is the current yield for a stock selling at 56.65 per share and paying a quarterly dividend of $0.60?

    a. 1.1 %

    b. 2.8 %

    c. 3.6 %

    d. 4.2 %

4. A shareholder buys 100 shares of a stock that then splits 3 for 1 and subsequently pays a 10% stock dividend. How many shares does the investor own after the split and stock dividend?

    a. 330

    b. 630

    c. 1,300

    d. 3,100

5. XYZ announces a cash dividend of $1.50 on Tuesday, April 12. The record date is Monday, May 2; the payment date is Thursday, June 16; and the ex-dividend date is Thursday, April 28. What is the first day that an investor can buy the stock and not receive this dividend?

    a. April 11

    b. April 28

    c. May 3

    d. June 16

PRACTICE EXERCISES

An investor wishes to purchase shares of Cyana Inc. (traded on Nasdaq). The company's next cash dividend is payable to shareholders of record on Thursday, April 10.

1. If an investor buys the stock, regular way, on Monday, April 7, when will she have to pay for the purchase?

2. Will this investor receive the forthcoming dividend?

3. What is the required holding period before the investor can sell the stock?

4. Who established the amount of the dividend?

5. Who set the ex-dividend date?

6. Who set the record date?

MULTIPLE-CHOICE ANSWERS AND EXPLANATIONS

1. **d.** The ex-dividend date is set two business days prior to the record date. The second business day before Wednesday, August 12 is Monday, August 10. One must be listed as a stockholder on the record date to receive the dividend.

2. **d.** The board of directors establishes dividend policy. Even preferred dividends have to be declared by the directors. A company is not bound by law to pay dividends, even if it is profitable.

3. **d.** The quarterly rate is $0.60, which works out to an annual rate of $2.40. The current yield is calculated by dividing the annual dividend by the current price: $2.40 / 56.65 = 4.2%.

4. **a.** The 3-for-1 split gives the shareholder 200 additional shares for a total of 300 shares; then the 10% stock dividend adds another 30 shares: 100 + 200 + 30 = 330.

5. **b.** The ex-dividend date is the first day that a buyer will not receive the forthcoming dividend. The stock must be purchased before the ex date to receive the dividend. Purchasers who buy on or after the ex date are not entitled to the dividend.

ANSWERS TO PRACTICE EXERCISES

1. Thursday, April 10

   The settlement date (when payment is due) is the third business day after the trade date. If there are no intervening holidays, stock trades effected on Monday settle that Thursday; Tuesday's trades settle that Friday; Wednesday's trades settle the following Monday; Thursday's trades settle the following Tuesday; Friday's trades settle the following Wednesday.

2. Yes, the investor will receive the dividend.

   With a record date of Thursday, April 10, the ex-dividend date will be set two business days earlier, Tuesday, April 8. Stock purchased before the ex-dividend date is entitled to the dividend.

3. There is no particular holding period.

   There is no such restriction. So long as a client is not "kiting" (buying stock with no intention of paying for it), stock may be sold immediately after being purchased.

4. The amount of the dividend was set by the company's board of directors.

5. The ex-dividend date was set by the NASD.

6. The record date was set by the company's board of directors.

CHAPTER 6

Corporate Bonds

Securities can be subdivided into two major categories: stocks (equities) and bonds (debt). When you purchase equity securities such as common and preferred stocks, you are considered to be a part owner of the company. When you buy debt securities such as bonds you are considered to have loaned money to the company. A bondholder has a creditor–debtor relationship with the company: The bondholder (creditor) has loaned the company (debtor) money. Equities represent ownership, bonds represent debt.

All corporations have common stock outstanding, and some have also issued one or more different classes of preferred stock. Most corporations also issue bonds to help finance their operations. Bonds differ from stocks in a number of important respects. Stocks pay dividends, but bonds pay *interest*. Just as all of a company's preferred stocks are senior to its common stock with respect to both dividend payments and rights in dissolution, that company's bonds are senior to both its preferred and common issues of stock. In theory, common and preferred issues go on forever (preferred issues may be called or converted, but they have no expiration date), while bonds have a limited life of from several to 30 years or more. Then they mature or come due for repayment. Stocks trade in dollars per share; corporate bonds trade in percentages of their par value.

Presuming that XYZ Corporation has only a single class of common stock but two different preferred issues outstanding, these securities might be referred to in the following manner: "XYZ" would refer to the company's common stock. "XYZ 8% pfd" and "XYZ 12% pfd" might be how the different preferred shares are designated. Notice that preferred issues have a longer, more descriptive name than common stock.

Most companies that have issued bonds have several different bonds outstanding at any given time, and we must also be able to distinguish among them. Here's how two of XYZ's bond issues might be referred to:

"XYZ 7s '08" and "XYZ 9s '12." These descriptions might also be written out in more detail, such as "XYZ 7% bonds maturing in 2008" and "XYZ 9% bonds maturing in 2012." The 7s is the same as 7%, and 9s means the same thing as 9%. The notation '08 stands for the year 2008, and '12 refers to the year 2012. Note that each bond's description shows, in addition to the corporate name (XYZ), two other pieces of information: the bond's *interest rate* and its *maturity date*.

INTEREST PAYMENTS

Bonds pay interest rather than dividends. Unlike most stocks that are on a four-times-a-year dividend payment schedule, bonds usually make their cash distributions twice each year. The interest rate that is part of a bond's description shows the percentage of the bond's par value that is paid annually. Since a bond is a loan, the amount of the loan—that is, the amount that the company must ultimately repay to the bondholder—is known as its *par value*. Just as stocks trade in shares, with 100 shares being considered a round lot, corporate bonds trade in $1,000 units (known as "one bond") with $10,000 worth (ten bonds) being considered a round lot. The bond's par value is also known as its face value. All bonds are paid off at their full face value when they mature.

Round Lot Trading Quantities

	# of Units	Usual Par Value of 1 Unit	Cost of 1 Round Lot at Par
Stocks	100	Varies	Varies
Corporate Bonds	10	$1,000	$10,000

An 8% bond pays interest in the amount of 8% of its par value each year. Presuming that we are referring to a single bond ($1,000 face value), then the annual interest would be $80 (8% of $1,000). Since the interest is paid in two equal semiannual installments, each of the two interest payment will be $40. The 8% interest rate is also known as the bond's *nominal yield* or its *coupon rate*.

A 12% bond pays $120 per year for each $1,000 of par value (12% of $1,000) in two semiannual payments of $60 each. The nominal yield on this bond is 12%, and we can also say that its coupon rate is 12%. One bond can be shown as "$1,000 par value," "$1,000 face value," or simply "1M." Ten bonds = $10,000 face value = $10,000 par value = 10M, and $100,000 worth of bonds would be written "100M."

The interest payments (also sometimes referred to as coupon payments) are made at six-month intervals. Sometimes the timing of these payments is shown by designating the two months of the year, and the day of the month, when the interest is paid: J&J1 means that the interest will be paid on the first days of January and July. The "J&J" can only refer to January and July, as neither January and June nor June and July are exactly six months apart. F&A stands for February and August, M&S refers to

March and September, A&O means April and October, M&N stands for May and November, and J&D signifies June and December. Many bonds, especially those issued more than several years ago, pay interest on either the first or the fifteenth of the month (F&A1 or J&D15), but in today's market almost any day of the month might be chosen. The bond's par value ($1,000 per bond) is usually repaid together with the final interest payment.

TYPES OF CORPORATE BONDS

Corporate bonds—bonds issued by corporations—are classified according to the type of collateral backing the bond. Just as you usually collateralize your bank loans (your new car is the collateral for the loan you took out to buy the car, and your home is the collateral for your mortgage), most bonds are also collateralized. *Mortgage bonds* are backed by some type of real property; *collateral trust bonds* are backed by other securities owned by the corporation; *equipment trust certificates* are backed by rolling stock or equipment such as trucks, airplanes, railroad cars, or oil drilling rigs; *debentures* are similar to signature loans in that no property is specifically pledged to back the loan. Debentures can be very solid, as when they are issued by a company with an excellent credit rating, or extremely speculative if they are issued by a company that does not have any unencumbered property to pledge.

PRICING CORPORATE BONDS

At first glance, most corporate bond prices look like high-priced stock quotes. Typical bond prices might be $92^1/_2$, $100^7/_8$, or $107^1/_8$. What must be understood is that each of these prices is expressed as a percentage of the bond's par value. A price of $92^1/_2$ for a bond translates to "$92^1/_2$% of par value."

Note: For the balance of these chapters on bonds, we show all illustrations of bond pricing and interest payments as if they were for just one bond—a single, $1,000 par value bond, or 1M.

$92^1/_2$% of $1,000 equals $925 (.925 × $1,000)
$100^7/_8$% of $1,000 equals $1,008.75 (1.00875 × $1,000)
$107^1/_8$% of $1,000 equals $1,071.25 (1.07125 x $1,000)

There's an easy way to convert these bond quotations into dollars and cents: Write out the bond price, converting the fraction to a decimal ($^1/_8$ = .125; $^1/_4$ = .25; $^3/_8$ = .375; $^1/_2$ = .50; $^5/_8$ = .625; $^3/_4$ = .75; $^7/_8$ = .875), and then move the decimal point one place to the right to show the dollar value of one bond (1M), two places to the right to indicate the dollar cost of ten bonds (10M), and three places to the right to show how many dollars one hundred bonds (100M) are worth. It's a two-step process: first write out the price with the fraction (if any) converted to a decimal, then move the decimal one, two, or three places to the right.

Bond Price	Fraction Expressed as a Decimal	Value of One Bond (1M) $1,000 Par	Value of Ten Bonds (10M) $10,000 Par	Value of One Hundred Bonds (100M) $100,000 Par
89$^1/_2$	89.50	$895.00	$8,950.00	$89,500.00
94	94.00	$940.00	$9,400.00	$94,000.00
99$^7/_8$	99.875	$998.75	$9,987.50	$99,875.00
100	100.00	$1,000.00	$10,000.00	$100,000.00
100$^1/_4$	100.25	$1,002.50	$10,025.00	$100,250.00
101	101.00	$1,010.00	$10,100.00	$101,000.00
101$^1/_8$	101.125	$1,011.25	$10,112.50	$101,125.00
103$^5/_8$	103.625	$1,036.25	$10,362.50	$103,625.00
108$^3/_8$	108.375	$1,083.75	$10,837.50	$108,375.00
111	111.00	$1,110.00	$11,100.00	$111,000.00
140$^3/_4$	140.75	$1,407.50	$14,075.00	$140,750.00

PREMIUM, PAR, AND DISCOUNT PRICING

The first three prices in the preceding table are all less than 100 and are known as *discount prices*. A price of exactly 100 is called *par*, and any prices above 100 (the last seven prices in the table) are *premium prices*. Bonds can trade at less than their face value (discount), at exactly their face value (par), or at more than their face value (premium). Bonds, like preferred stocks, are usually issued at or very near to their par values, and they always mature at their par values. Bonds are issued at par in the primary market. They might very well trade in a wide price range during their life on the secondary market, but they always mature at par.

CALLABILITY AND CONVERTIBILITY

Some bond issues are callable and some are convertible. The principles are exactly the same as for callable and convertible preferred stocks, described in Chapter 4.

BOND RATINGS

Several professional organizations rate corporate and municipal bonds with respect to the ability of their issuers to make regular interest payments and to repay the face value at maturity. Well-rated bonds are considered safer than those with lower ratings. Two of the best-known rating services are Moody's and Standard & Poor's. Their ratings, from highest quality on down, are:

	Moody's	Standard & Poor's
Investment	Aaa	AAA
Grade	Aa	AA
Bonds	A	A
	Baa	BBB
High-Yield /	Ba	BB
Junk Bonds	B	B
	Caa	CCC
	Ca	CC
	C	C

Some ratings go down to the D's for very speculative issues. Also, sometimes the ratings listed above are slightly modified by adding additional signs or letters such as +, −, 1, 2, or 3. Bonds in the top four ratings (Aaa through Baa and AAA through BBB) are known as *investment grade* or *bank quality bonds*, and are suitable for inclusion in most fixed-income portfolios. Bonds rated Ba or BB or lower are known as *junk bonds*. Also known as *high-yield bonds*, junk bonds are certainly more speculative than investment-grade issues, but they yield considerably more to compensate, at least in part, for their additional risk.

INTEREST-RATE SENSITIVITY

Like the prices of preferred stocks, the market prices of bonds react inversely to changes in interest rates. When interest rates go up, bond prices go down, and when interest rates go down, bond prices go up. Buyers must beware of paying too much more than face value for a bond with a relatively high coupon rate if that bond is callable. Even though most callable bonds are called at a slight premium, it is dangerous to pay more than that premium if the bond might be called.

As with convertible preferred stocks, convertible bonds tend to run with the underlying common stock. If the common stock goes way up in price, so will the convertible bond, low yield or not. Many newspaper listings that show the current yields for nonconvertible bonds do not show the yields for convertible bonds, possibly because they acknowledge the fact that convertible bond prices may be more closely tied to the action of the underlying stock rather than to interest rates.

	Corporate Bonds	Preferred Stock	Common Stock
Voting Rights	No Voting Rights	Does Not Vote	May Vote
Callable	May Be Callable	May Be Callable	Not Callable
Convertible	May Be Convertible into Common Stock	May Be Convertible into Common Stock	Not Convertible
Dividends	Fixed Interest Payment	Fixed Dividend	Variable Dividend
Seniority of Payments	Priority over Preferred Stock	Priority over Common Stock	Lowest Claim to Dividend
Seniority in Dissolution	Priority over Preferred Stock	Priority over Common Stock	Lowest Claim in Dissolution

SUMMARY

Bonds are senior to both common and preferred stocks and, in general, are safer than stocks. They are fixed-income debt securities that pay interest twice each year. The major categories of bonds are corporate (issued by corporations, as are stocks), municipal (issued by states, cities, and other political subdivisions), and government (issued by the U.S. government). Bonds have a maturity date, up to about 30 years after issuance, at which time they will repay their par value to investors. Bonds are sensitive to changes in interest rates. Some bond issues are callable, some are convertible. Most corporate and municipal bonds are rated by several agencies. Nonconvertible (straight) bonds are generally purchased for the relatively safe, dependable, and predictable income they provide. Bonds are conservative investments, especially suited to income-oriented investors and those unwilling to assume large risks.

MULTIPLE-CHOICE QUIZ

Use the following information to answer all five questions:

XYZ 8% debentures mature in 2020. They pay interest F&A15. They are trading at $107^1/_2$.

1. What is the nominal yield of the bonds?
    a. 8%
    b. more than 8%
    c. less than 8%
    d. cannot be determined

2. Interest payments will be made on:
    a. February 1 and April 15
    b. February 15 and April 15
    c. February 1 and August 15
    d. February 15 and August 15

3. An owner of 10 bonds (10M) would receive annual interest of:
    a. $8
    b. $80
    c. $800
    d. $8,000

4. How much would 100 bonds (100M) cost at the price indicated?
    a. $1,075
    b. $10,750
    c. $107,500
    d. $1,075,000

5. The collateral for these bonds is:
    a. rolling stock
    b. other stocks and bonds
    c. a mortgage on real property
    d. unspecified

PRACTICE EXERCISES

Mr. James Treanor has the following corporate bonds in his portfolio:

10M	($10,000 par value)	ABC Corp.	8%	@ 102.00
10M	($10,000 par value)	CDE Corp.	9%	@ 106.50
100M	($100,000 par value)	DEF Corp.	7.5%	@ 92.75
100M	($100,000 par value)	EFG Corp.	12%	@ 122.63

1. What is the total market value of his bond holdings?

2. What is the total amount of annual interest that Mr. Treanor will receive from these bonds?

3. If interest rates rise sharply, what effect might this have on the market value of Jim's bond portfolio?

MULTIPLE-CHOICE ANSWERS AND EXPLANATIONS

1. **a.** Nominal yield is simply the bond's interest rate, also known as its coupon rate. Nominal yield has nothing to do with a bond's market price or length to maturity.

2. **d.** F&A15 can only stand for February 15 and August 15. February is the only month beginning with the letter F and August is six months after February. Even though 15 is only written out once, it indicates that day for both months.

3. **c.** 8% of $10,000 is $800 (.08 x 10,000). The owner of 10 bonds would receive two $400 payments each year, one on the 15th of February and another on the 15th of August.

4. **c.** 100 bonds at 107 1/2 are worth $107,500. The first step is to write out the bond's quoted price with the fraction expressed as a decimal (107.50); then move the decimal point three places to the right, so 107.50 becomes 107500 or $107,500. Answer a is the value of one bond (1M) at the price shown, answer b shows the value for 10 bonds, and answer d indicates the market value of 1,000 bonds (1MM).

5. **d.** Debentures do not have any specifically named collateral. Choice a is the collateral for equipment trust certificates, choice b for collateral trust bonds, and choice c for mortgage bonds.

ANSWERS TO PRACTICE EXERCISES

1. $236,230

The bonds are worth, respectively:

ABC—$10,200 (10 × $1,020)

CDE—$10,650 (10 × $1,065)

DEF—$92,750 (100 × $927.50)

EFG—$122,630 (100 × $1,226.30)

The total comes to $236,230.

2. $21,200

Each year the bonds will pay, respectively:

ABC—$800 (8% × $10,000)

CDE—$900 (9% × $10,000)

DEF—$7,500 (7.5% × $100,000)

EFG—$12,000 (12% × $100,000)

The total comes to $21,200.

3.   The bond portfolio's market value would decline sharply.

When interest rates rise, the prices of fixed-income securities decline. When interest rates decline, the prices of fixed-income securities rise.

CHAPTER 7

Municipal Bonds

Bonds issued by state and local governments are known as *municipal bonds*. The interest payments on all municipal bonds used to be exempt from federal taxation, and these bonds were once known as "tax-exempts." A change in the tax law in the mid-1980s divided municipal bonds (financial industry personnel refer to them as "munis") into two categories, at least insofar as the tax status of their interest payments is concerned: private purpose bonds, whose interest payments are generally taxable, and public purpose bonds, which pay interest free from federal taxation and sometimes also free from state and local taxation.

Private purpose bonds are generally considered to include those issues giving 10% or more of their benefit to private activities such as sports arenas; public purpose bonds are used to finance what are considered to be essential public services such as libraries and highways.

TAX STATUS OF INTEREST PAYMENTS

The interest on public purpose bonds (most muni issues are public purpose bonds) is free from federal taxation and sometimes free from state taxation as well. An investor who buys muni bonds issued within the "home" state would not normally pay any state tax on the interest payments. If Mary Brown resided in New Jersey and purchased New Jersey Turnpike bonds, she would pay neither federal nor state (New Jersey) tax on the interest she received. However, if Mary bought West Virginia Turnpike bonds, she would still not be liable for federal tax on her interest payments, but she might very well have to pay state tax (New Jersey) on them.

It is important to realize that the tax exemption some munis enjoy on their interest payments does *not* apply to capital gains. If you sell a municipal bond for more than its purchase price, you have a capital gain. Such gains on all types of municipal bonds are fully taxable, just like the capital gains you might have on any other type of security. The tax-exempt status of certain municipal bonds extends only to their interest payments.

TAXABLE EQUIVALENT YIELD

Broadly speaking, municipal bonds are attractive for high-tax-bracket investors who are seeking income. The tax-free nature of the interest payments on most public purpose bonds makes them very desirable for such investors. This tax exemption is so important that often a wealthy investor will retain more after-tax money on a municipal bond holding than on another investment with a higher yield. There is a simple formula that takes into account the tax-free nature of the interest payments and permits investors to compare the after-tax return on both munis and fully taxable bonds such as corporates. If an investor in the 30% tax bracket is considering investing in a municipal bond with a yield of 5%, she should know that a taxable bond would have to yield 7.14% to give her the same after-tax return! Here's the arithmetic: Divide the tax-free yield (the yield on the muni) by 1 minus the investor's tax bracket; this shows the *taxable equivalent yield*. In our example, 5.00% / 1–.30 = 5.00% / .70 = 7.14% This demonstrates that for an investor in the 30% tax bracket, a 5% yield on a tax-exempt bond is equivalent to a 7.14% yield on a taxable bond. For this particular investor, a taxable yield of less than 7.14% on a taxable bond would not be as appealing as the 5% tax-free yield.

Municipal bonds are not considered suitable investments for most retirement plans, such as IRAs, because investments in such plans are sheltered from taxation anyway. Munis are, however, among the last remaining true "tax shelters" and they are widely held by wealthy investors. The underlying reason that many munis are accorded tax exemption is that the federal government recognizes the essential needs that such financing satisfies, and local governments are thus able to borrow at lower interest rates. Corporate bonds usually have the highest returns, then government bonds, with munis affording the lowest apparent returns.

The fact that munis yield less than government bonds, despite their greater risk, underscores the value investors place on the tax-exempt status of their interest payments.

	Yield	Equivalent Taxable Yield
Corporate Bond	10%	10%
Government Bond	6%	6%
Municipal Bond	5%	7.1%*

*Assuming investor is in the 30% federal tax bracket.

GENERAL OBLIGATION BONDS AND REVENUE BONDS

Municipal bonds that are backed by the full faith and credit of a municipality are known as *general obligation bonds* (GOs). Such bonds are usually fairly safe because they are secured by the municipality's ability to tax. There are good and bad GOs, of course, but as a class they are well regarded and fairly safe, and do not yield as much as other types of munis that are riskier. That is a constantly recurring theme with all fixed-income securities: The more highly regarded the bond—the higher its rating—the lower its yield will be. If an investor is seeking a relatively safe investment, the cost of that safety is a lower return. There is no free lunch in the world of investing. If you want safety, you cannot also expect to receive a high yield.

Bonds used to finance public works such as bridges and turnpikes are known as *revenue bonds*. Their debt service (interest and principal payments) is supported by the income from the facility, not by taxes. A turnpike's income comes from the tolls collected and the franchise fees it receives from the service stations and restaurants at its rest areas. The business (in this case, the turnpike) has to carry the bond. The state the turnpike traverses is not responsible for making interest or principal payments; the road stands or falls by itself. Revenue bonds as a class are certainly less secure than GOs, but there are often high-quality revenue bonds that are safer than poorly-rated GOs. Sometimes a state will cosign for a revenue bond issue by promising to make good on any missed payments. This of course makes the revenue bond much safer. Such bonds are known as *double-barreled bonds*.

REGISTERED BONDS

Ownership of many municipal bond issues may be demonstrated by an actual certificate, similar to the certificates issued for stocks. If the bond certificates have the owner's (bondholder's) name or his brokerage firm's name on them, they are said to be *registered bonds*. If an investor purchases bonds, pays for them in full, and then asks his brokerage firm to send the bonds to him, the broker will register the bonds in the owner's name before shipping them to the owner. The purchaser of the bonds is the *beneficial* (actual) owner of the bonds and, if the bond certificates are registered in his name, he is also the *registered* owner (owner of record).

STREET NAME

If the owner wants the brokerage firm to retain physical possession of the bonds, then the bonds are registered in the broker's name. The investor is still the owner of the bonds (beneficial owner), but the brokerage firm is the bondholder of record (registered owner). The broker is simply holding the bonds for the client, who still retains full ownership. Certificates that belong to the customer but are registered in the broker's name are said to be in *street name*.

With very few exceptions, stocks and bonds that are sent to customers are registered in the customers' names—the customers are both the beneficial owners and the registered owners. Stock and bond certificates that are held for customers by a brokerage firm are held in street name—the customers are the beneficial owners but the broker is the registered owner.

COUPON BONDS

Municipal bonds were once commonly offered in another format known as *coupon bonds*. Such bonds do not have the owner's name on them, either the bondholder's name or the broker's name. That's why they are also known as *bearer bonds*—they are assumed to be the property of the person or institution possessing the bonds. This is not an odd concept when you consider that the dollar bills in your purse or wallet are also bearer instruments; your name is not on them, but that does not pose a problem. Bearer bonds do not have to go through a transfer process when they change hands, because there are no owners' names to change. This makes the job of delivering bonds after a sale much easier and cheaper; they are simply handed over from the seller to the buyer.

Coupon bonds are physically much larger than registered bonds because they have a number of coupons attached to the certificate. The coupons are about 1 inch by 3 inches and there is a different coupon for each of the bond's interest payments. When a 20-year coupon bond was issued there were 40 coupons attached, one for each of the two interest payments that were to be made during each of the bond's 20 years of life. A 15-year coupon bond was issued with 30 coupons, and so forth. These sheets of coupons were directly attached to the bond and had to be cut off to be cashed in. Every six months the bondholder would cut off the appropriate coupon (the coupons were individually dated and numbered) and cash it or deposit it at a bank—that's the way the bondholder would collect the interest. Sometimes well-to-do people are referred to as "coupon clippers." This slang expression describes those whose lifestyle is supported by clipping the interest coupons from the bonds that they own.

When the last coupon is paid, the owner surrenders the bond itself to collect the face amount. Investors holding coupon bonds must safeguard them carefully because if they are stolen, they can be sold by the thieves fairly easily, just as they might steal and dispose of stolen cash. Coupon bonds were once prevalent, and their impact on the nomenclature of the bond market still prevails; it is common to refer to a bond's interest rate as its "coupon" rate, and the dates on which interest payments are made (J&J1, F&A15) are called "coupon payment" dates.

When a coupon bond is sold, it must of course be delivered to the buyer. To make a "good delivery" (acceptable for payment), the bond must have all its unpaid coupons attached. If someone were to sell, in mid-January of 2003, a coupon bond with interest payment (coupon payment) dates of March 1 and September 1 (M&S1), then he must deliver the bond with the next coupon (March 1, 2003) and all the subsequent coupons attached. This is expressed in financial trading terms as "3/1/03 & SCA" (the March 1, 2003 and all Subsequent Coupons Attached).

Even though coupon bonds are no longer being issued, they will be around until the last-issued bonds mature in about the year 2010. The word *coupon* will always be with us.

THE MUNICIPAL SECURITIES RULEMAKING BOARD

In 1975 the latest *self-regulatory organization* (SRO) was created, the Municipal Securities Rulemaking Board (MSRB). Other SROs include the major security and commodity exchanges and the National Association of Securities Dealers (NASD). Self-regulatory organizations enforce fair and ethical trade practices in the security and commodity industries. All SROs are under the jurisdiction of other agencies such as the Federal Reserve and the Securities and Exchange Commission (SEC). The MSRB is charged with overseeing the municipal bond industry, but it has no enforcement authority. While it makes all the rules, it looks to either the NASD or banking authorities to perform any required enforcement.

SERIAL BONDS AND TERM BONDS

Many municipal bond offerings are quite complex in that a number of different bonds of the same issuer are brought to market at the same time. There may be many different small issues (up to 15 or so) maturing at intervals of from one year to about fifteen years from the date of issue. These small issues, from several hundred thousand dollars to several million dollars, are known as *serial bonds*. Each one is a separate issue with a different maturity date. Often the new offering also includes one or several larger issues (many millions of dollars of par value) maturing after the last serial issue. These larger, longer issues are known as *term bonds*. When both serial and term bonds are issued at the same time, the issue is known as a split offering.

Pricing Term Bonds

Term bonds are priced similarly to corporate bonds, that is, as a percentage of their par value, in eighths. Term bond prices might look like this: $97\frac{1}{4}$, 99, $100\frac{3}{8}$, 102, $104\frac{1}{2}$. Such quotes can be converted to dollars and cents by expressing any fractions in decimal fashion and then moving the decimal point one place to the right for a single bond ($1,000 par value—1M), two places to the right for ten bonds ($10,000 par value—10M), and three places to the right for 100 bonds ($100,000—100M). The actual value of 10M bonds trading at $97^1/_4$ is $9,725; 10M at 99 is $9,900; 100M at $100^3/_8$ equals $100,375; 100M at 102 equals $102,000; and 1MM (one million dollars par value) at $104^1/_2$ is worth $1,045,000. Review Chapter 6 for details on converting quotations to dollar values.

A round lot for municipal bonds is $100,000 worth (100M). The secondary market traditionally has wide spreads (differences between bid and asked prices), especially for smaller amounts of bonds (odd lots).

Pricing Serial Bonds

Serial bonds are usually priced on a yield basis. Instead of quoting prices as a percentage of par value (as for corporate bonds and municipal term bonds), they are quoted on the basis of their yield to maturity. (Yield to maturity is explained at length in Chapter 10.) Such prices might show as 5.07, 6.12, or 7.25. The prices quoted mean that the first bond (5.07) is trading at a dollar price that will give an investor a yield on that investment of exactly 5.07%; the next quotation shows a yield of 6.12%; the final quote is for a yield of 7.25%. Buyers of these bonds are not interested in the exact dollar price they are going to pay, but rather are interested in the yield they will receive on their investment. Quoting on a yield basis takes into account the bond's length to maturity, its coupon rate, and its actual dollar cost. Many buyers, especially institutional buyers, are primarily interested in the return the bond will give them; they are not interested in details. These buyers do not care whether the bond is trading at a premium or a discount. They simply want to know what their actual return will be, and this is what a yield basis price shows.

	Serial Bonds	Term Bonds
Issue	Small issues with multiple maturity dates	Large issues with fewer, longer maturity dates
Quoted	Yield to Maturity (YTM)	Percent of Par

SUMMARY

Municipal bonds traditionally afford wholly or partially tax-free interest payments. The municipal bond market is huge, with about 1,500,000 different issues outstanding. Divided into GOs and revenues, munis are used to develop local infrastructure and public services. Some municipal bonds are supported by property taxes and other levies, and others are supported by tolls or fees. Munis can be attractive investments, particularly for individuals in the higher tax brackets. Some municipal bonds are insured against default, and any insured bonds that do default will be purchased from investors at par. Insured bonds have a high degree of safety but do not yield as much as uninsured bonds. Quoted either as a percentage of par or on a yield basis, municipal bonds traditionally yield less than U.S. government bonds, not because they are higher in quality but because of the tax-exempt status of their interest payments.

MULTIPLE-CHOICE QUIZ

1. Which type of municipal bond does not pay tax-exempt interest?
   a. toll road bonds
   b. school district bonds
   c. private purpose bonds
   d. public purpose bonds

2. An investor is in the 28% tax bracket and is considering investing in a tax-exempt municipal bond yielding 6.00%. To enjoy the same after-tax yield on a corporate bond the investor would have to buy a bond yielding:
   a. 5.0 %
   b. 8.3 %
   c. 11.7 %
   d. 20.0 %

3. A round lot of municipal bonds is considered to be:
   a. 100 shares
   b. 10,000 shares
   c. 10 bonds
   d. 100 bonds

4. $100,000 par value (100M) of municipal bonds trading at $98^1/_8$ are worth:
   a. $981.25
   b. $9,812.50
   c. $98,125.00
   d. $981,250.00

5. Municipal term bonds are usually quoted:
   a. as a percent of par, in eighths
   b. on a current yield basis
   c. on a yield to maturity basis
   d. in dollars and cents

PRACTICE EXERCISES

An investor in the 20% tax bracket is considering the purchase of general obligation bonds, at par, issued by the state in which he resides. The GOs have an interest rate of 5.25%. He is also considering the purchase, also at par, of the same principal amount of 6.25% corporate bonds issued by the BYO Corporation. BYO is also incorporated in the investor's home state.

1. Which issue, the municipal bond or the corporate bond, will afford the investor the greatest after-tax yield?

2. Which issue would be better suited for inclusion in the investor's IRA account?

MULTIPLE-CHOICE ANSWERS AND EXPLANATIONS

1. **c.** Choices a and b clearly are issued for the benefit of the general public and as such enjoy tax exemption. Private purpose bonds, such as for sports arenas, cannot pay tax-exempt interest.

2. **b.** The taxable equivalent yield is found by dividing the tax-exempt yield by 1 minus the investor's tax bracket.

    $6.00 / 1 - .28 = 6.00 / .72 = 8.3\%$

3. **d.** Choice a is a round lot for stocks. Trades of more than 10,000 shares of stock are referred to as block trades. Choice c indicates a round lot for corporate bonds.

4. **c.** First write out the quoted price, expressing the fraction as a decimal (98.125). Then move the decimal three places to the right to establish the dollar value of 100 bonds ($100,000 par value or 100M) at that price. Thus, 98.125, with the decimal moved three places to the right, becomes 98125., or $98,125. Choice a shows the value of one bond (1M), choice b shows the value of 10 bonds (10M), and choice d indicates the value of a million dollar's worth (1MM).

5. **a.** Term bonds are quoted like corporate bonds, in eighths as a percentage of par. They are sometimes called *dollar bonds*. Choice c is how serial bonds are quoted. Term bonds are issued in large amounts and for fairly long maturities, and thus are relatively more likely to be owned by individuals rather than institutions. This is the probable reason that they are quoted like corporates, so the general public can more easily understand their pricing.

ANSWERS TO PRACTICE EXERCISES

1.   The municipal bond will give him the greater after-tax yield.

Dividing the tax-exempt yield by 100% minus the investor's tax bracket gives the taxable equivalent yield: 5.25 / 100% − 20% = 5.25 / .80 = 6.56%.

This indicates that, for an investor in the 20% tax bracket, a corporate bond would have to offer a yield of 6.56% to compare with the tax-free yield of 5.25% afforded by the muni.

There is no particular tax exemption for interest paid on corporate bonds of a company incorporated in the investor's home state.

2.   The corporate bond

Interest payments received in IRA accounts are not taxed at the time of receipt, whether paid on taxable or tax-free bonds, so there is no particular tax advantage for munis in an IRA or other tax-sheltered retirement account.

CHAPTER 8

U.S. Government Securities

The most creditworthy of all debt instruments are issued by the Treasury Department of the United States. Also known as "Treasuries" or "governments," they are backed by the full faith and credit (and the taxing power) of the government. Such securities are unrated, as they are considered to be beyond the risk of default on interest or principal. These super-safe securities are excellent for investors who demand ultimate safety and who are willing to accept the relatively low yield they afford.

TAX STATUS

The interest paid on governments is fully taxable for federal purposes, but not subject to state and local taxation. Any capital gains resulting from trading in governments *is* taxable.

To recap the taxation of the major types of bonds: Any *capital gain* resulting from trading in corporate, municipal, or government bonds is taxable. The *interest* on such bonds is fully taxable for interest received from corporate bonds (taxable by both federal and state); generally nontaxable for interest from municipal bonds (nontaxable federal and state); and partially taxable for interest from government securities (taxable by the federal government, but not taxable by the state).

Tax Status of Bonds

	Local	State	Federal
Interest on Corporates	Taxable	Taxable	Taxable
Interest on Municipals	Generally Nontaxable	Generally Nontaxable	Generally Nontaxable
Interest on Treasuries	Generally Nontaxable	Generally Nontaxable	Taxable
Capital Gains	Taxable	Taxable	Taxable

BOOK-ENTRY SECURITIES

Physical bonds, bonds that exist as paper securities, may be in registered or bearer (coupon) format. Many bonds are no longer issued in either of these forms, or in fact in any form at all. Such bonds are known as *book-entry securities*. The owner merely receives periodic statements from the brokerage firm through which the securities were purchased. It's very similar to receiving a statement from a bank where you have a checking or savings account. While you are long the securities, you will receive a statement attesting to that fact. The account will remain long until you either transfer the account to another institution or sell the securities, or until the securities mature.

This arrangement is very popular with the brokerage community, because it saves a great deal of paperwork (there isn't any paper) and time.

SAVINGS BONDS

One of the best-known government securities is the *savings bond*. Series EE savings bonds, available in denominations of from $50 to $10,000, are issued at one-half their face value (a deep discount) and mature at full face value. They do not make periodic payments, as their interest is effectively paid in one lump sum when the bonds are cashed in about 10 years after purchase. This is the *zero-coupon bond* principle. The yield on EE bonds is reset several times a year in accordance with the yields on other government securities. There is an established minimum yield that has varied from about 4% to $7^1/2$% in recent years. EE bonds can be held well beyond their maturity and will continue to earn interest. Taxes on the interest may be paid annually as the interest accrues, or may be paid in one lump sum at maturity. Individuals are limited to purchases of no more than $15,000 ($30,000 face value) of EE bonds in any one year.

HH bonds, which make regular interest payments during their life, are similar to the more traditional corporate bonds. HH bonds can be acquired only in exchange for maturing EE bonds and pay interest semiannually at a slightly lower rate than EE bonds. Savings bonds are considered nonmarketable in that they can only be redeemed, not resold in the secondary market. Early redemption results in lower yields. Savings bonds are usually purchased through banks or payroll savings plans, not through brokers.

The U.S. Treasury began issuing inflation-indexed bonds—I bonds—late in 1998. Earnings on these bonds are based on a combination of two rates—a fixed rate and a variable inflation rate that is adjusted twice a year to reflect changes in the Consumer Price Index. In the event of a negative CPI (less than zero), the bonds will not decline in value. As with EE bonds, I bonds must be held for at least six months. There is a penalty for redemption within five years of purchase. I bonds may be purchased in denominations ranging from $50 to $10,000.

MARKETABLE GOVERNMENT SECURITIES

The three types of marketable government securities are Treasury bills, Treasury notes, and Treasury bonds. These securities are very actively traded in the secondary market.

Treasury bills are issued at a discount from their full face value, with maturities of either three months, six months, or one year. The three-month (90-day) bills and the six-month (180-day) bills are sold at auction every week; the one-year bills are offered monthly. Treasury bills are noncallable and are only offered and traded at a discount. Like savings bonds, they do not pay interest regularly. The interest earned by the holder is simply the difference between the discounted purchase price and the full face value that is paid at maturity. T-bills are priced on a discounted yield basis rather than as a percentage of their par value. A quotation on a Treasury bill might be: "5.08 bid, 5.06 asked." This means that if an investor were able to buy at the bid price, he would receive a discounted yield of 5.08%, while if he paid the asked price (a higher price), his yield would be only 5.06%. This is another example of the fact that the higher the price, the lower the yield! Some publications show a coupon equivalent yield as well, so investors can better compare the discounted yield on T-bills with the more traditional yield to maturity on T-notes and T-bonds. Treasury bills are available in denominations of from $10,000 to $1,000,000. A round lot of T-bills is $5,000,000.

Treasury notes are issued with maturities of one to ten years. They have a fixed coupon and pay interest twice a year. They are noncallable and are traded as a percentage of their par value. Because they are traded in much larger blocks than corporates or munis (a T-note round lot is $1,000,000), they are quoted in thirty-seconds (32nds) rather than eighths (8ths). Government security traders need to use a quote system in which the bid and asked prices are closer together than $1/8$. To illustrate: If two traders are $1/8$ apart on a round lot of corporate bonds (10M)—$99^1/2$ bid offered at $99^5/8$—the difference between the two prices is $12.50. Ten bonds at $99^1/2$ are worth $9,950.00, and 10 bonds at $99^5/8$ are worth $9,962.50. That's not too great a dollar difference. But if those two traders were dealing with a T-note or T-bond round lot (1MM), that same $1/8$ difference would be $1,250! That amount is worth haggling over. To narrow the spread, government note and bond traders use 32nds (and sometimes 64ths) rather than eighths so they can get closer together on price. T-note prices might be written as 99:16, 101:03, or 104:28. These prices would be referred to as "99 and 16 thirty-seconds," "101 and 3 thirty-seconds," and "104 and 28 thirty-seconds." Note that the figure to the right of the colon in a T-note or T-bond quotation refers to 32nds.

Treasury bonds are issued with maturities of from more than 10 years to about 30 years. Like T-notes, they have a fixed rate of interest, make periodic payments, and are quoted as a percentage of their par value, in 32nds. Some

T-bonds are callable. The callable issues are usually shown with a "double" maturity date. The "Nov 02-07 $7^7/_8$" bonds have a final maturity of 2007 (07) but are callable beginning in the year 2002 (02). Some financial publications show T-note and T-bond prices with a hyphen rather than colon just before the 32nds—113-16 rather than 113:16. Both quotations mean 113 and 16 thirty-seconds. Interestingly, $113^{16}/_{32}$ is mathematically equivalent to $113^1/_2$, and works out to $1,135 for a single (1M) bond. A corporate bond worth that amount ($1,135) would be quoted as "$113^1/_2$"while a T-bond or T-note worth exactly that same dollar amount would be quoted as "113:16." The yield quoted on a callable Treasury bond will be calculated to the call date if the bond is trading at a premium (above 100), but will be calculated to the final maturity date if the bond is trading at a discount. This gives the potential buyer a worst-case scenario yield.

	T-Bills	T-Notes	T-Bonds
Issued At	Discount	Par Value	Par Value
Term to Maturity	Up to 1 year	1–10 years	10 + years
Callable	No	No	Some
Round Lot	$5,000,000	$1,000,000	$1,000,000
Quotes	Discounted Yield	Priced in 32nds	Priced in 32nds

PRICING TREASURY NOTES AND TREASURY BONDS

Converting quotations to dollars is a two-step process, similar to the method utilized with corporate bond quotations (see Chapter 6). Write out the price with the number of 32nds (if any) expressed as a decimal, then move the decimal two places to the right for 10 bonds ($10,000), three places for 100 bonds ($100,000), and four places for $1,000,000 worth of bonds (1MM).

Decimal Equivalents for 32nds

:01 = $^1/_{32}$ = .03125   :17 = $^{17}/_{32}$ = .53125

:02 = $^2/_{32}$ = .0625   :18 = $^{18}/_{32}$ = .5625

:03 = $^3/_{32}$ = .09375   :19 = $^{19}/_{32}$= .59375

:04 = $^4/_{32}$ = .1250   :20 = $^{20}/_{32}$ = .6250

:05 = $^5/_{32}$ = .15625   :21 = $^{21}/_{32}$ = .65625

:06 = $^6/_{32}$ = .1875   :22 = $^{22}/_{32}$ = .6875

:07 = $^7/_{32}$ = .21875   :23 = $^{23}/_{32}$ = .71875

:08 = $^8/_{32}$ = .2500   :24 = $^{24}/_{32}$ = .7500

:09 = $^9/_{32}$ = .28125   :25 = $^{25}/_{32}$ = .78125

:10 = $^{10}/_{32}$ = .3125   :26 = $^{26}/_{32}$ = .8125

:11 = $^{11}/_{32}$ = .34375   :27 = $^{27}/_{32}$ = .84375

:12 = $^{12}/_{32}$ = .3750   :28 = $^{28}/_{32}$ = .8750

:13 = $^{13}/_{32}$ = .40625   :29 = $^{29}/_{32}$ = .90625

:14 = $^{14}/_{32}$ = .4375   :30 = $^{30}/_{32}$ = .9375

:15 = $^{15}/_{32}$ = .46875   :31 = $^{31}/_{32}$ = .96875

:16 = $^{16}/_{32}$ = .5000

10 bonds ($10,000 par value) at 101:04 would cost $10,112.50.

100 bonds ($100,000 par value) at 99:26 would cost $99,812.50.

$1,000,000 par value (1MM) at 102:15 would cost $1,024,687.50.

GOVERNMENT AGENCY BONDS

There are a number of government-sponsored issues that are not direct obligations of the United Sates, but they do have some kind of federal guarantee or sponsorship. Generally referred to as *agencies*, they traditionally yield more than Treasuries, and are also traded in 32nds. Agencies include:

Federal National Mortgage Association (FNMA), "Fannie Mae"

Government National Mortgage Association (GNMA), "Ginnie Mae"

Student Loan Marketing Association, "Sallie Mae"

Federal Home Loan Banks (FHLB), "Freddie Mac"

Federal Land Banks (FLB)

Federal Farm Credit International Bank for Reconstruction and Development (World Bank)

Inter-American Development Bank

SUMMARY

U.S. government securities offer ultimate safety of principal as they are free of the risk of default. These debt obligations range in maturity from three months to more than 30 years. They trade very actively in the secondary market (except for EE, HH, and I bonds).

Treasury bills do not pay coupons and are quoted on a discounted-yield basis. They are noncallable and can never trade at a premium. Treasury notes, bonds, and agencies trade as a percentage of their par value, in 32nds. They can trade at premiums or discounts, and make regular interest payments. The interest on most of these securities is exempt from state tax, but not exempt from federal tax. A round lot for T-notes and T-bonds is $1,000,000; a round lot for T-bills is $5,000,000. The Federal Reserve primarily uses Treasury bills in its open market operations to regulate the money supply.

MULTIPLE-CHOICE QUIZ

1. Arrange the following in order of their length to maturity at the time they are initially issued, shortest maturity first.

   I   Treasury notes
   II Treasury bills
   III Treasury bonds

   a. II, III, I
   b. I, II, III
   c. III, I, II
   d. II, I, III

2. Capital gains on Treasury bond trades are:

   a. taxable by the federal government but not by the state
   b. taxable by the state but not by the federal government
   c. taxable by both state and federal governments
   d. nontaxable by either the state or federal government

Use the following information to answer the next three questions.

A newspaper listing for a U.S. government bond reads:

$$\text{Aug } 03\text{-}08 \; 8^3/_8 \; 117{:}24 - 117{:}30 - 03 \; 5.89$$

3. 100 bonds at the offer price will be worth:

   a. $11,730
   b. $11,793.75
   c. $117,300
   d. $117,937.50

4. Which two of the following are correct?

   I   The bonds are callable.
   II The bonds are noncallable.
   III Their yield is 8.375%.
   IV Their yield is 5.89%.

   a. I and III
   b. I and IV
   c. II and III
   d. 11 and IV

5. The previous day's bid price was:

   a. 117:21
   b. 117:27
   c. 117:33
   d. cannot be determined

PRACTICE EXERCISES

What is the dollar value for each of the following Treasury notes?

1. 100M @ 100:16

2. 250M @ 99:08

3. 1MM @ 97:24

4. How would an investor be taxed on the interest income from such notes?

5. How would the investor be taxed on any capital gain from the Treasury notes?

6. Might these issues of Treasury notes be callable?

MULTIPLE-CHOICE ANSWERS AND EXPLANATIONS

1. **d.** Bills have maximum maturities of one year, notes have maximum maturities of 10 years, and bonds mature in more than 10 years.

2. **c.** Capital gains are fully taxable. The interest on Treasuries is also taxable by the federal government, but not by state governments.

3. **d.** The fraction $^{30}/_{32}$ expressed as a decimal is .9375. The quoted price, with the appropriate fraction, is 117.9375. Moving the decimal three places to the right gives 117937.5—or 117,937.50—for 100 bonds (100M); 10 bonds (10M) at that price are worth $11,793.75.

4. **b.** The double maturity date (03-08) shows that the bonds are due in 2008, but may be called beginning in 2003. The nominal yield (the coupon rate) is 8.375%, but the yield is shown as 5.89%. Since the bond is trading at a premium (above par), the yield shown is the yield to call.

5. **b.** The net change for the day is shown as "–03," which signifies down $^{3}/_{32}$. If the bid shown is 117:24, and it's down $^{3}/_{32}$ from the previous day, then the previous day's bid was 117:27.

ANSWERS TO PRACTICE EXERCISES

1. $100,500

   $100{:}16 = 100^{16}/_{32} = 100^1/_2 = \$1005$

   $100 \times \$1005 = \$100,500$

2. $248,125

   $99{:}08 = 99^8/_{32} = 99^1/_4 = \$992.50$

   $250 \times \$992.50 = \$248,125$

3. $977,500

   $97{:}24 = 97^{24}/_{32} = 97^3/_4 = \$977.50$

   $1,000 \times \$977.50 = \$977,500$

4. The interest will be taxable by the federal government, but not taxable by the state. The same situation obtains for Treasury bills, Treasury bonds, and savings bonds.

5. Capital gains are fully taxable.

   While interest on municipal bonds and Treasury issues may be fully or partially exempt from tax, *all* capital gains earned outside a tax-sheltered account such as an IRA are fully taxable.

6. The notes are not callable.

   Treasury bills and Treasury notes are never callable; some Treasury bonds are callable.

CHAPTER 9

Interest Payments

Many stocks pay dividends. All debt securities pay interest in one form or another. The interest on savings bonds and zero-coupon bonds is paid all at once, when they mature. Most other debt instruments make periodic interest payments (coupon payments) on a twice-a-year schedule. Zero-coupon bonds are attractive to investors who have no need for a continuous stream of income during the period of time it takes the bond to mature. Such investors are thus relieved of the necessity for reinvesting their interest payments. For investors who require a continuing income stream, bonds that pay interest regularly are more appropriate.

CALCULATING INTEREST PAYMENTS

Most bonds' descriptions include their interest rate and maturity. An issue described as the "XYZ 8.25s of '27" indicates a bond with an interest rate of 8.25% (8.25s) and a maturity in the year 2027 ('27). This bond might also be described as: XYZ $8^1/4$% bonds due in 2027.

This issue will pay, annually, interest amounting to $8^1/4$% of the bond's face value. Assuming an investor owns just a single bond ($1,000 face value, or 1M), she will receive $82.50 per year in interest. Since the interest will be paid to her in two equal semiannual installments, each of the payments will be for $41.25. The annual interest is thus $8^1/4$% of the bond's face value, or $8^1/4$% of $1,000 (.0825 × $1,000).

The simplest way to calculate the actual payout is to write out the interest rate (the coupon rate), expressing any fraction as a decimal, and then move the decimal one place to the right for one bond (1M), two places for 10 bonds (10M), and three places for 100 bonds (100M). To find the annual interest for $1,000 par value (one bond) of the XYZ $8^1/4$s '05, write out the interest rate, showing the fraction as a decimal. This converts "8$\frac{1}{4}$" to 8.25. Moving the decimal one place to the right gives 82.5, or $82.50 annual interest for 1 bond (1M). The annual interest on 10 bonds (10M) would be $825, and the interest for one year on 100 bonds (100M) would be $8,250.

The annual interest on 10 ABC 9% bonds would be $900 (9.00 with the decimal moved two places to the right becomes 900, or $900). The annual interest on 100 YAC 7$\frac{1}{4}$s would be $7,250; the interest rate, in decimal format, is 7.25, and moving the decimal three places to the right gives 7250 or $7,250.

Interest payments continue for the life of the bond. If that life is shortened because the bond is redeemed or otherwise canceled, interest payments will cease. Among the reasons for a bond not reaching its full maturity date are that the bond has been converted into common stock by its owner (like certain preferred stocks, some bonds are convertible), or the bond has been called by the issuing corporation. The payment of interest due on a company's bonds is senior to the payment of dividends on that same company's common or preferred stocks so, at least in that respect, that company's bonds are safer than its preferred or common stocks. All U.S. government securities are free from the risk of default, but there is some degree of risk with municipal bonds and corporate bonds. The bond rating systems (see Chapter 6) assess that risk.

ACCRUED INTEREST ON CORPORATE AND MUNICIPAL BONDS

When a cash dividend is pending on a stock, the stock trades either with the dividend (cum dividend) or without the dividend (ex-dividend). To receive an upcoming dividend, you must purchase the stock before the ex-dividend date (see Chapter 5). Cash dividends are never shared between stockholders—either one person or the other receives the full amount. Interest-paying bonds, with a few exceptions, *do* share their payments between buyer and seller. Each receives a portion of the upcoming interest payment. This is the principle of *accrued interest*. The seller of a bond is entitled to receive interest up to, but not including, the settlement date of the sale. Since the seller is not entitled to actually receive the proceeds of the sale until settlement date, then it is logical that he is entitled to receive interest prior to that date. On the settlement date, the buyer is charged for the purchase and so he (the buyer) is entitled to receive interest beginning on that date.

The brokerage community simplifies the mathematics for determining accrued interest on corporate bond and municipal bond trades. Accrued interest calculations for such debt instruments are made using 30-day months and 360-day years. The actual number of days in a given month is not used, as every month is assumed to be 30 days long. The year is considered to be 360-days in length (12 months of 30 days each) rather than 365 or 366 days. Since the buyer will be the holder of the bond when it will make its next payment, he will receive the full payment, but is only entitled to part of it. Instead of receiving the full payment and then rebating the appropriate portion to the seller, the buyer pays—on settlement date—the seller's portion, the accrued interest. The seller receives his interest at the time of the sale (it comes from the buyer, who is prepaying that interest to him), and the buyer will receive the complete coupon payment on the next interest payment date. This pays back the buyer for the accrued interest he paid out on settlement date, leaving him with his fair share.

Think of this process like starting a new job in midweek. You prepay half a week's wages to the person whose job you are taking over, and then receive a full week's pay at the end of the week. The former employee was entitled to half a week's pay, and you paid him this. You were entitled to the other half of the pay, and that is what you wound up with; you paid out half a week's pay and received a full week's pay. Each of you received what you were entitled to.

Here's an example: James Treanor buys one ABC 9% bond from Steve Bradley on Monday, March 5. Steve has owned the bond for several years and has been receiving interest regularly. The ABC bonds are "J&J1," meaning that their interest is paid on the first of January and the first of July. The bond pays a total of $90 annually (9% of $1,000), in two semiannual installments of $45 each. The trade of March 5 will settle on March 8 (three business days later), so Steve is entitled to receive interest from the last coupon date before the sale (January 1) up to, but not including, the settlement date of the trade. Steve should receive interest for the entire months of January and February, and for the first 7 days of March. The number of days of accrued interest totals 67—30 days for January, 30 days for February, and 7 days for March. The formula is: number of days of accrued interest multiplied by the annual interest, then divided by 360.

Plugging in the numbers from the example—67 × $90 / 360—the accrued interest comes to $16.75. This accrued interest will be charged to Jim Treanor and paid to Steve Bradley. Steve will receive the $16.75 from Jim, who will be reimbursed when the next coupon is paid.

ACCRUED INTEREST ON
U.S. GOVERNMENT NOTES AND BONDS

Since the average government bond trade is substantially larger than most corporate and municipal bond trades, it is appropriate that the calculation of accrued interest for governments be more exact than for other bonds. Just as corporates and many munis are traded in eighths while governments are traded in thirty-seconds, there is also a difference in the calculation of accrued interest. Corporates use 30-day months and 360-day years, while governments use actual days (months of 28, 29, 30, or 31 days and 365- or 366-day years). The calculation for accrued interest on governments is further refined in that only one-half the amount of the annual interest and one-half of the interest period are used in the formula.

Another difference is that government bonds settle on the first business day following the trade date, not on the third day after as do corporates and munis. The calculation is much more complex than for corporates. Here is the procedure: First, determine the number of days from the previous coupon date through the day before settlement, and then divide this number by the total number of days in the half-year during which the trade took place. The final step is to multiply by a single coupon payment (one-half the annual interest).

Example: Andrew Barthman purchases $100,000 par value (100 bonds) of U.S. Treasury 6s on Tuesday, March 14, 1999. The bonds pay interest on January 1 and July 1 (J&J1). The trade will settle the next business day, March 15. Mr. Barthman must pay accrued interest from the date of the most recently paid coupon before the trade (January 1, 1999) through the day before settlement. Since the trade settles on March 15, he must pay interest through March 14. The total number of days of accrued interest will be 73. He owes for the entire months of January and February, and for the first 14 days in March. January—31 days; February—28 days (1999 was not a leap year so February had 28 days); March—14 days. Thus, 31 + 28 + 14 = 73 days accrued interest. Next we must calculate the total number of days in the entire half-year period from the date of the last-paid coupon to the next coupon date. Since the trade was done in March, the half-year we are concerned with is the period from January 1 to July 1. (If the trade took place in the latter half of the year, we would instead calculate the number of days from July 1 to the following January 1.) The total number of days in the first half of 1999 is 181 (January, 31; February, 28; March, 31; April, 30; May, 31; June, 30). Then 31 + 28 + 31 + 30 + 31 + 30 = 181. The last number we need to calculate is half a year's interest on the bond. The $100,000 par value of bonds with a 6% interest rate pay $6,000 annually, and half this amount, $3,000, is paid every six months. The formula is:

$$\frac{\text{Number of days of accrued interest} \times \text{one-half annual interest}}{\text{\# of days between last coupon and next coupon}}$$

Substituting, we get:

$$\frac{73 \times \$3,000}{181} = \frac{219,000}{181} = \$1,209.94 \text{ accrued interest}$$

Do not be concerned if you have a difficult time mastering these rather arcane formulas. The important thing is to appreciate the general concept of accrued interest, rather than the specific mathematics.

TRADING FLAT

Accrued interest is added to the majority of bond trades for corporate, municipal, and government bonds. Bonds that do not trade with accrued interest include zero-coupon bonds, income (adjustment) bonds, and bonds already in default. Zero-coupon bonds don't pay interest regularly; income bonds pay interest only when it's earned; and defaulted bonds aren't paying their current coupons. All these bonds are said to be trading *flat*, or without accrued interest. Income bonds are sometimes received in exchange for other bond issues when a company gets into financial trouble. These bonds are similar to cumulative preferred stock and will pay interest only when, and if, it is earned.

SUMMARY

Most bonds pay interest twice yearly. A bond's description usually includes its interest rate—the coupon rate—as well as the year of its maturity. Coupon payment dates are six months apart. Bonds that trade without accrued interest include zero-coupon issues, income (adjustment) bonds, and issues already in default. These bonds are said to trade flat. Accrued interest is calculated through the day before settlement, using 30-day months and 360-day years for corporate and municipal bonds and actual days for government bond transactions. Accrued interest is paid by the buyer of the bond to the seller of the bond, and is an added cost of the purchase. Investors receive their interest either by submiting coupons from their bearer bonds to a bank or by payment directly from the issuer on registered bonds.

MULTIPLE-CHOICE QUIZ

Use the following information to answer all five questions:

An investor purchases 10 ($10,000 par value) NFW 6s of '05 at 98 on Friday, June 10. Interest payment dates are M&N1.

1. How much interest will the investor receive each year?
    a. $60
    b. $98
    c. $600
    d. $980

2. On what date will the trade settle?
    a. June 10
    b. June 11
    c. June 15
    d. June 17

3. How many days of accrued interest will be added?
    a. 40
    b. 44
    c. 100
    d. 106

4. What is the amount of the accrued interest?
    a. $73.33
    b. $84.02
    c. $103.31
    d. cannot be determined from the information presented

5. Presuming the trade will be done on a net basis (no commission charge), what will be the total amount paid for the bonds?
    a. $9,873.33
    b. $9,884.02
    c. $9,903.31
    d. cannot be determined from the information presented

PRACTICE EXERCISES

1. What amount of accrued interest will be added to a purchase of 10M ($10,000 par value) of 9% corporate bonds purchased on Wednesday, October 4? The bonds are J&J1.

2. If the bond in question 1 was purchased at 101.05 net by John Deere, what will be the total amount he must pay?

3. What will be Mr. Deere's tax-cost basis?

4. What amount of accrued interest will be added to a purchase of 1MM ($1,000,000 par value) of 7% Treasury bonds purchased on Friday, August 7? The bonds are M&N15.

MULTIPLE-CHOICE ANSWERS AND EXPLANATIONS

1. **c.** The 6% coupon rate is multiplied by the total par value of the bonds involved; 6% of $10,000 is $600 (.06 × 10,000). An alternative way to do the calculation is simply to express the coupon rate in decimal form and then move the decimal four places to the right for 10 bonds (or three places for one bond or five places for 100 bonds): 6% = .06, and moving the decimal four places to the right gives 600. or $600.

2. **c.** The trade settles three business days after the trade date. It's a trade in NFW bonds, a corporate bond, not a Treasury issue. The third business day after Friday, June 10 is Wednesday, June 15. Do not forget to account for the weekend.

3. **b.** Interest accrues from the coupon date before the trade date through the day before settlement. An "M&N1" bond pays interest on the first of May and November. The trade was done in June, so the previously-paid coupon was May 1. Settlement day is June 15, so June 14 is the day before settlement. The buyer is owed interest for the month of May—30 days—and for 14 days in June, for a total of 44 days of accrued interest.

4. **a.** The answer is found by multiplying the days of accrued interest by the total annual interest and then dividing by 360: 44 × $600 / 360 = $26,400 / 360 = $73.33

5. **a.** Ten bonds at 98 are worth $9,800. Adding the accrued interest gives "final money" of $9,873.33.

ANSWERS TO PRACTICE EXERCISES

1. $245

The bonds pay interest January 1 and July 1. The last-paid coupon prior to the trade was July 1, therefore the seller is owed interest from that date through the day before settlement. A trade on Wednesday, October 4 settles on Monday, October 9 (T+3). The seller is due interest for the full months of July, August, and September (at 30 days per month), and the first 8 days in October: 30 + 30 + 30 + 8 = 98 days. The annual interest on 10M 9% bonds is $900 ($10,000 × 9%).

When calculating accrued interest on corporate and municipal bonds, we use a 360-day year. The accrued interest formula is: $900 × 98 / 360 = $245.

2. $10,350

"Final money" consists of both the principal amount ($10,105) and the accrued interest ($245).

3. $10,105

His tax-cost basis does not include the accrued interest, only the principal amount.

4. $16,548.91

The bonds pay interest May 15 and November 15. The last-paid coupon prior to the trade was May 15, therefore the seller is owed interest from that date through the day before settlement. A trade on Friday, August 7, settles on Monday, August 10 (T+1). The seller is due interest for part of May, the full months of June and July (using the actual number of days in each month), and the first 9 days in August: 17 + 30 + 31 + 9 = 87 days. Since we begin counting on May 15, there are 17 days of accrued interest in May, counting from the 15th through the 31st, inclusive. There are a total of 184 days in the half-year in which the bond was traded (May 15 / November 15): May—17 (see above), June—30, July—31, August—31, September—30, October—31, November—14 = 184 days in the half-year.

The annual interest on 1MM of 7% bonds is $70,000 ($1,000,000 × 7%). We use only half a year's interest when figuring the accrued interest on a government bond. The accrued interest formula for the government bond is: $35,000 × 87 / 184 = $16,548.91.

Yield Calculations

Most bonds are purchased for their interest income rather than for their growth prospects. Investors must be able to measure the return on fixed-income investments so as to be able to properly compare one such investment with another. This chapter is devoted to several different methods of measuring return.

Bonds may trade at par, at premium prices, or at discount prices. They are issued with a bewildering array of different coupon rates, and their maturities may be imminent or many years in the future. With all these different factors, it is rarely obvious which investment offers the higher return. Bond A may have a higher coupon than bond B, but A may be selling at a higher price!

NOMINAL YIELD

A bond's *nominal yield* is simply its coupon (interest) rate. The ABC 8s of '08 have a nominal yield of 8.00% (8s). The DEF $9^1/_2$s of '09 have a nominal yield of 9.50% ($9^1/_2$s). A bond's nominal yield does not take into consideration its market price or time to maturity. The ABC 8s, for example, have a nominal yield of 8.00% whether they are trading at par, at a discount, or at a premium, and whether they are due to mature in one year or in 20 years. Nominal yield is synonymous with coupon rate.

CURRENT YIELD

Common stocks do not have a nominal yield because their dividends vary, but dividend-paying stocks do have a current yield. *Current yield* is calculated by dividing the security's annual dividend or interest by its current market price. If XYZ Corporation pays an annual dividend of $1.20 on its common stock, and that stock is currently trading at 20, its current yield is 6.0% ($1.20 / 20 = .06). An investor paying $20 a share for the stock will receive back, each year, 6% of the amount he has invested. His return (yield) is 6.0%, as that portion of his investment is being returned to him each year as a dividend. If the dividend were to be raised to $1.40 per year and the stock's price remained at 20, the current yield would then be 7.0% ($1.40 / 20 = .07). If the dividend stayed at $1.20 and the stock rose in value to 24.50, the current yield would be 4.9% ($1.20 / 24.50 = .049). A security's current yield changes as either its annual income or its current price changes.

There are two weaknesses inherent in the quoted current yield of a common stock. The current yield calculation often uses the stock's anticipated annual income. While analysts are very good at estimating the coming year's dividend, the company's board of directors has the power to change the dividend—raising it, lowering it, or even eliminating it altogether—which will certainly affect the current yield quoted to the investor at the time of purchase. An even more important influence is the uncertainty about the stock's future price. If GHI common stock was trading at 28.50 while it was paying dividends at the annual rate of $2.20, it would be said to have a current yield of 7.7% ($2.20 / 28.50 = .077). This would be small consolation to the purchaser of the stock, even though she did receive the entire $2.20 in dividends over the year following her purchase, if at the end of that year the stock had declined to 18 per share. Yes, she would have received $2.20 in dividends, but her stock would be down $10.50 per share, which would result in an overall loss.

When dealing with fixed-income securities such as preferred stocks and bonds, current yields may be considered to be less misleading than common stock current yields in that the annual income is known in advance and will not change. Preferred stocks pay fixed dividends and bonds pay fixed interest rates. The current yield calculation thus has a constant numerator (the number above the line in the equation), unlike the changing dividend rate on a common stock. There still remains the problem of changing prices, which we shall address a little later. Here are two examples of current yields on bonds. [See Chapter 6 to review converting a 6% bond's coupon rate (6s) to its $60 annual payout and its quoted price of 94$^{1}/_{2}$ to a dollar value of $945.]

GHI 6s of '99, trading at $94^1/_2$, have a current yield of 6.3% ($60 / $945 = .063).

JKL $8^1/_4$s of '04, trading at 105, have a current yield of 7.9% ($82.50 / $1,050 = .079).

The GHI bonds have a nominal yield of 6.0% and the JKL bonds have a nominal yield of 8.25%. Note that the GHI bonds that are trading at a discount (less than $1,000) have a current yield that is greater than their nominal yield. The JKL bonds, trading at a premium (more than $1,000), have a current yield that is less than their nominal yield.

The higher the price, the lower the yield and the lower the price, the higher the yield. This is a very important concept. Customer A buys a bond with a 9% nominal yield when it is newly issued at par. He receives $90 per year and has paid $1,000 for the bond. At the time of purchase, his current yield was 9.0% ($90 / $1,000 = .09), the same as the nominal yield. If that issue of bonds then goes down in price to 93 and is purchased by customer B, the new buyer's current yield will be 9.7% ($90 / $930 = .097). Customer B's bond will also have a nominal yield of 9.0%. If, some time later, those bonds rise in price to $104^3/_4$ and are then purchased by customer C, his current yield will be 8.6% ($90 / $1,047.50 = .086). Again, customer C's bond still has a nominal yield of 9.0%.

It makes sense when you realize that all three buyers receive the same amount of interest, but they invested different amounts of money. If customer B bought at a discount, her yield would naturally be higher than customer A's, because she paid less to receive the identical interest payments. Customer C, who paid the most of all, gets the lowest return of all. B bought at a discount (the bond was on sale) and C bought at a premium. The only time a bond's nominal yield and its current yield are the same is when the bond is trading exactly at par ($1,000 per bond), as it was when purchased by A.

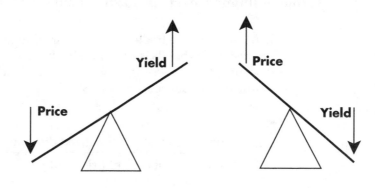

YIELD TO MATURITY

The most professional measurement of a bond's yield is its *yield to maturity*. This is the rate of return an investor will realize by holding an interest-bearing security until it matures. This calculation takes into account the purchase price, the redemption price, the nominal yield, and the length of time to maturity, and also factors in the time value of money and the assumption that all coupon payments are reinvested at the yield-to-maturity rate. Confused? Take comfort in the fact that yield to maturity (YTM) is a mystery even to many experienced Wall Street professionals. All cash flows are taken into account. If you hold a bond until it matures, you are effectively "selling" it at par ($1,000) at maturity. If a bond is held until it matures, there are no surprises, because you know the current price of the bond, the amount and timing of all coupon payments, and the "sale" price and time ($1,000 at maturity). You know every penny that will go into the investment (the purchase price) and every penny that will come out of the investment (the coupon payments and the repayment of par value when the bond matures). Professional investors always use YTM rather than current yield, as YTM factors in any premium or discount that will add to or subtract from the dollars earned through the interest payments.

Yield to maturity can be found by using either a yield basis book or a specialized calculator. Both the yield book and the calculator will give you the same, accurate figure. YTM can be *approximated* by the relatively simple rule-of-thumb method, using only a simple calculator or even longhand arithmetic. The rule-of-thumb method for bonds trading at a discount is: The numerator (the number above the division line) is the bond's annual interest plus the annualized discount. The denominator (the number below the division line) is the average of the bond's purchase price and its par value. The formula is: annual income + annualized discount divided by average of current price and par. Here is an example of the calculation of the rule-of-thumb yield to maturity for a discount bond.

JKL 9% bonds are trading at 92 and are due to mature in 10 years. The annual interest on 9% bonds is $90. Since the bond is trading at 92 ($920), it has an $80 discount ($1,000 − $920). This discount, divided by the number of years to maturity (annualized), equals $8 ($80 / 10). Plugging in the numbers, we have:

$$\frac{\text{Annual interest} + \text{Annualized discount}}{\text{Average of current price and par}} = \text{Yield to Maturity (rule of thumb)}$$

$$\frac{90 + 8}{(920 + 1{,}000) \, / \, 2} = \frac{98}{960} = 10.2\% \text{ Yield to Maturity (rule of thumb)}$$

This compares with the actual yield to maturity, taken from the basis book, of 10.3%—not bad for a simplified method. Note that the YTM in the foregoing example, 10.3%, was higher than the bond's nominal yield of 9%, and also higher than its current yield of 9.8% ($90 / $920 = .098). This is the pattern for bonds trading at a discount—the current yield is always higher than the nominal yield (because fewer dollars have to be invested to earn the coupon), and the yield to maturity is higher still, reflecting the fact that at maturity the investor will receive full par value for an investment of less than par. In effect, the buyer of a discount bond who is willing to hold the bond until it matures has two sources of income—the coupon payments that will be received every six months, and the "extra" money that will be received at maturity. The extra money is the difference between the purchase price and full par value. In the previous example, the investor paid only $920 for the bond but will ultimately receive $1,000. The yield-to-maturity calculation factors in this additional gain.

The yield-to-maturity calculation for premium bonds differs only slightly. Instead of adding the annualized premium to reflect the gain resulting from buying at a discount and ultimately receiving par, one must *subtract* the annualized premium. If you pay more than par for the bond and only receive par at maturity, you are effectively buying high and selling low, losing the difference. The formula is:

$$\frac{\text{Annual interest} - \text{Annualized premium}}{\text{Average of current price and par}} = \frac{\text{Yield to Maturity}}{\text{(rule of thumb)}}$$

YAC bonds, 9% coupon, are trading at 106 and are due to mature in 5 years. Their rule-of-thumb yield to maturity is 7.6%:

$$\frac{90 - 12}{(1,060 + 1,000) / 2} = \frac{78}{1,030} = 7.6\% \text{ Yield to Maturity} \atop \text{(rule of thumb)}$$

The annualized discount that we subtracted from the annual interest was derived by dividing the premium ($1,060 − $1,000) by the number of years to maturity: $60 / 5 = 12. The actual yield to maturity from the basis book is 7.54%, remarkably close to the figure we arrived at by the rule-of-thumb method. YAC bonds, trading at a premium, have a nominal yield of 9%, a current yield of 8.5% ($90 / $1,060), and a yield to maturity of 7.5%. Note the pattern: Since these are premium-priced bonds, their current yield is less than their nominal yield and their yield to maturity is lower still. Compare this with discount bonds.

YIELD TO CALL

Investors must always be quoted the *lowest* yield to maturity on a callable bond. If a callable bond is selling at a discount and it is called, the investor will immediately receive at least par, $1,000, even though she had paid less than par. As an example, if Joan Bradley buys an 8% MNO bond due in 10 years at 90, and the bond is called soon thereafter at par, she has an almost immediate windfall of at least $100, the difference between her purchase price ($900) and the call price ($1,000 or more). Joan would make a large profit on her investment, over 11%, even if she never collected a coupon. She would have bought for $900 and almost immediately "sold" for $1,000 or more—not a bad deal. Joan cannot count on the bond being called, so she can only be quoted the bond's yield to maturity, which is 9.5%. It would not be fair to suggest that her yield is going to be any higher than that because there is no certainty that the bond will be called at all. Mrs. Bradley must be shown the lower yield to maturity rather than the higher yield to call.

Contrast this with a situation in which a client purchases a premium-priced callable bond. Mrs. Rosemary Monaghan buys NFW 12% bonds, due in 10 years, at 106½. She paid a premium because she was attracted by the bond's high coupon rate and its current yield of 11.3% ($120 / $1,065 = .113). The bond's yield to maturity is 11.0%. But what if the bond were callable, at par, beginning one year after Rosemary purchased it? She would lose the premium, $65, in one year rather than over the 10 years to the maturity date. She would not have had time to have the coupon payments, over a 10-year period, offset the premium. She loses the premium in just one year, but does not receive all the coupons. Mrs. Monaghan must be warned against this possibility by being shown the much lower yield to call (5.3%) rather than the yield to maturity. Again, the customer must be shown the worst-case scenario.

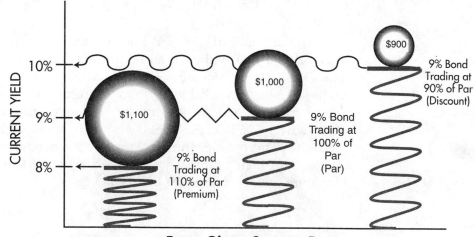

**For a Given Coupon Rate,
the Higher the Price, the Lower the Yield.**

BASIS POINTS

Differences between yields are expressed in *basis points*. A basis point is 1/100th of 1% of yield (0.01%). A yield of 6.07% is 2 basis points higher than a yield of 6.05%. The difference between a 7.00% yield and a 7.25% yield is 25 basis points. A yield of 9.00% is 100 basis points (a full percentage point) higher than a yield of 8.00%.

SUMMARY

Because bonds are purchased primarily for their interest payments rather than for their growth prospects, it is important to understand the principles of yield—the investor's return. A bond's nominal yield is simply its coupon rate, and is unchanged over the life of the bond. Nominal yield is not affected by a bond's market price or its length to maturity. Current yield is found by dividing a bond's annual interest payments by its current price. Premium bonds have current yields that are lower than their nominal yields, and discount bonds have current yields that are higher than their nominal yields. Yield to maturity is the method used by professionals, and it factors in the premium or discount. Yield to call is used for callable bonds selling at a premium.

MULTIPLE-CHOICE QUIZ

Use the following information to answer the first three questions:

NFW debentures have an 11% coupon rate and will mature in 12 years. They are currently trading at 103.

1. What is the bond's nominal yield?
   a. 10.7%
   b. 11.0%
   c. 11.3%
   d. cannot be determined without knowing the interest payment dates

2. What is the bond's current yield?
   a. 10.7%
   b. 11.0%
   c. 11.3%
   d. cannot be determined without knowing whether the bond is callable, and at what price

3. What is the bond's rule-of-thumb yield to maturity?
   a. 10.4%
   b. 10.6%
   c. 10.8%
   d. 11.0%

Answer questions 4 and 5 using the following information:

PQR 8% bonds are trading at 104 and are due to mature in 7 years.
STU 10$^3/_8$% bonds are trading at 97 and are due to mature in 6 years.
Do not use a calculator to answer either question.
Do not use pencil and paper.
Try to arrive at the correct answers by reasoning only.

4. The PQR bonds have a current yield of:
   a. 7.7%
   b. 8.1%
   c. 8.5%
   d. 8.9%

5. The STU bonds have a yield to maturity of:
   a. 9.8%
   b. 10.1%
   c. 10.3%
   d. 10.7%

PRACTICE EXERCISES

Maxim Corporation 7% bonds are trading at 92.00. They are due to mature in 10 years and are currently callable at 101.75.

1. What is the current yield on the Maxim bonds?

2. What is the rule-of-thumb yield to maturity on these bonds?

3. Will the yield to call be greater or less than the yield to maturity?

Calabrese Corporation 9% bonds are trading at 105.50. They are due to mature in five years. They are callable at par.

4. What is the current yield on Calabrese bonds?

5. What is the rule-of-thumb yield to maturity on these bonds?

6. Will the yield to call be greater than or less than the yield to maturity?

Utilize the Bond Yield Table provided to answer questions 7 to 10. Calculate *yields* to two decimal places (8.82%, 11.03%). Calculate bond *prices* to the nearest cent ($1,009.63, $991.88).

7. What is the yield to maturity for a $10^3/_4$% bond, maturing in 11 years, that is trading at 97.50?

8. What is the price of a $10^3/_4$% bond maturing in 10 years, that is being offered on a 10.11 basis?

9. What is the yield to maturity for a $10^3/_4$% bond, maturing in $11^1/_2$ years, that is trading at 109.00?

10.   What is the price of a 10³/₄% bond, maturing in 13 years, that is being offered on an 11.10 basis?

10³/₄%   **Years to Maturity**

PRICE	8	9	10	11	12	13
96.00	11.53	11.47	11.43	11.40	11.37	11.35
96.50	11.43	11.38	11.34	11.31	11.29	11.27
97.00	11.33	11.29	11.26	11.23	11.21	11.19
97.50	11.23	11.20	11.17	11.15	11.13	11.12
98.00	11.13	11.11	11.09	11.07	11.05	11.04
98.50	11.04	11.02	11.00	10.99	10.98	10.97
99.00	10.94	10.93	10.92	10.91	10.90	10.90
99.50	10.85	10.84	10.83	10.83	10.83	10.82
100.00	10.75	10.75	10.75	10.75	10.75	10.75
100.50	10.66	10.66	10.67	10.67	10.68	10.68
101.00	10.56	10.58	10.59	10.59	10.60	10.61
102.00	10.38	10.40	10.42	10.44	10.45	10.47
103.00	10.19	10.23	10.26	10.29	10.31	10.33
104.00	10.01	10.06	10.11	10.14	10.17	10.19
105.00	9.83	9.90	9.95	9.99	10.02	10.05
106.00	9.66	9.73	9.80	9.84	9.89	9.92
107.00	9.48	9.57	9.64	9.70	9.75	9.79
108.00	9.31	9.41	9.49	9.56	9.61	9.66
109.00	9.14	9.25	9.35	9.42	9.48	9.53
110.00	8.97	9.10	9.20	9.28	9.35	9.40

MULTIPLE-CHOICE ANSWERS AND EXPLANATIONS

1. **b.** Nominal yield is simply the coupon rate (the bond's rate of interest).

2. **a.** Annual interest divided by current price gives current yield. Annual interest is $110 (11%) and current price is $1,030 (103); thus, $110 / $1,030 = .107 or 10.7%.

3. **b.** The premium is $30 ($1,030 – $1,000) which, divided by the 12 years to maturity, annualizes to $2.50 ($30 / 12 = $2.50). That amount is subtracted from the annual interest and becomes the equation's numerator ($110 – $2.50 = $107.50). The denominator is the average of the current price and par ([$1,030 + $1,000] / 2 = $1,015). Then, $107.50 / $1,015 = .106 or 10.6%. Note that this is a premium bond. The highest of the three yields should be the nominal yield, next the current yield, and then the yield to maturity; and that's the way they stack up—nominal yield 11.0%, current yield 10.7%, and yield to maturity 10.6%.

4. **a.** This is a premium bond, therefore the bond's current yield and its yield to maturity must both be lower than its nominal yield. The nominal yield (the coupon rate) is 8%, so the current yield must be less than 8%. No math is necessary, as the only yield shown that is less than 8% is answer a.

5. **d.** This question uses the same reasoning as question 4. The bond is trading at a discount, so its current yield and its yield to maturity must be greater than its nominal yield. The nominal yield is 10.375% ($10^{3}/_{8}$s) so the correct answer must be a larger figure. Only answer d fills the bill.

ANSWERS TO PRACTICE EXERCISES

1. 7.61%

    A 7% bond pays $70 annually; a bond priced at 92.00 sells for $920.

    $$\frac{\$70}{\$920} = 7.61\%$$

2. 8.13%

    To the numerator we add the annualized discount: ($1,000 – $920 / 10) or $8. The denominator is the average of the purchase price and par: ($920 + $1,000 / 2) = $960.

    $$\frac{\$70 + \$8}{\$960} = \frac{\$78}{\$960} = 8.13\%$$

3. The yield to call will be greater than the yield to maturity.

    The yield to call is always greater than the yield to maturity for bonds trading at a discount.

4. 8.53%

    A 9% bond pays $90 annually; a bond priced at 105.50 sells for $1,055.

    $$\frac{\$90}{\$1,055} = 8.53\%$$

5. 7.69%

    From the numerator we subtract the annualized premium: ($1,055 – $1,000 / 5) or $11. The denominator is the average of the purchase price and par: ($1,055 + $1,000 / 2) = $1,027.50

    $$\frac{\$90 - \$11}{\$1,027.50} = \frac{\$79}{\$1,027.50} = 7.69\%$$

6. The yield to call will be less than the yield to maturity.

    When callable at par, the yield to call is always less than the yield to maturity for bonds trading at a premium.

7. 11.15%

   Read *down* the "11-year" column and *across* the "97.50" row. The answer is found where the column and row intersect.

8. $1,040

   Read *down* the "10-year" column to the figure 10.11, then read *across* to the left to the price column that reads 104.00. This price, in dollars, equals $1,040.

9. 9.45%

   The average of the 11-year yield (9.42%) and the 12-year yield (9.48%) is 11^1/$_2$ years.

10. $976.25

    Set up a proportion between the next higher and the next lower *yields*, and the next higher and the next lower *prices*.

    11.12% = 97.50

    11.04% = 98.00

    The difference between 11.12 and 11.04 is .08. The difference between 97.50 and 98.00 is .50. The spread between the known yield of 11.12 and the yield of 11.10 that we are seeking is .02. The proportion sets up this way:

    $$\frac{.02}{.08} :: \frac{x}{.50}$$

    $$x = .125$$

    We must add this amount (.125) to 97.50 to arrive at the interpolated price of 97.625 (97.50 + .125). A bond priced at 97.625 = $976.25.

Investment Companies

Among the most popular investments available in the United States are various types of investment companies. These firms pool the assets of many different individuals sharing similar investment objectives. A professional investment team, for a fee, operates a portfolio that is owned by a large number of investors. The individual investors each own their separate "piece of the action" in proportion to their holdings of the entire investment fund. It's a package-plan approach to investing.

ADVANTAGES OF INVESTMENT COMPANIES

When a person purchases one of these funds, he owns a percentage of the entire portfolio of securities—a small piece of every stock and every bond owned by the fund—which affords him greater *diversification* than he would receive by investing directly in only a few different stocks or bonds. Investment companies typically own dozens or even hundreds of different securities, so an investor is not subject to the same risk he would face if he purchased only one or a few securities.

The securities in the pooled account are under the full-time supervision of a professional money management team that makes all the decisions as to which securities to buy, which securities to sell, and when to take profits and losses. The presumption is that these professionals will do a better job than could individual investors acting on their own. The professionals are experienced in managing investment funds and are adept at placing orders, hedging, and reacting appropriately to business news and economic conditions—skills that are well beyond those of the average investor. The *professional management* thus afforded is another compelling reason for the enormous popularity of investment companies.

There are a number of attractive options available to purchasers of investment companies, particularly to those who purchase the open-end type (described later). Investments can be made in relatively modest amounts. It is possible to arrange for regular purchases through automatic withdrawals from a checking account. The investment company handles all bookkeeping and recordkeeping chores and reports regularly to shareholders so they may easily keep track of their fair share of the pooled fund's dividends, interest, and capital gains. These are a few of the attributes that contribute to an investment company's *convenience* as an investment medium.

The principal reasons for the enormous popularity of investment companies are the major benefits they provide: diversification, professional management, and convenience.

NET ASSET VALUE

It is a fairly simple matter to find out the true worth of investment company shares. Their assets consist only of securities and cash, and usually all their holdings have an easily determined market value. The fund managers simply add up the current market values of all the securities in the portfolio plus any cash held, subtract any liabilities such as accrued management fees, and then divide by the number of fund shares outstanding. This gives *net asset value* per share, sometimes simply referred to as *NAV*. NAV is the underlying value of a share of the fund—its liquidating value or its book value. If the fund were to be liquidated, each investor would receive the per-share net asset value for each fund share he or she owned.

$$\frac{\text{Total assets} - \text{Total liabilities}}{\substack{\text{Number of mutual} \\ \text{fund shares outstanding}}} = \text{Net Asset Value (NAV)}$$

$$\frac{\$40,000,000\ (\text{TA}) - \$2,000,000\ (\text{TL})}{\substack{3,800,000 \\ \text{fund shares outstanding}}} = \text{Net Asset Value (NAV)}$$

$$\frac{\$38,000,000\ (\text{Net assets})}{3,800,000\ \text{shares}} = \$10.00/\text{share (NAV)}$$

The fund's NAV is a running total of the actual net value of each fund share. A fund's net asset value changes in direct relationship to how well or how poorly that fund's portfolio of securities performs in the market. If the value of the securities rises, so does the fund's NAV; the NAV falls if the portfolio decreases in value. The NAVs of investment companies are published regularly in the financial press, usually once a week for closed-end funds and daily for open-end funds. These two major subcategories of investment companies are described in the next several sections.

CLOSED-END FUNDS

Also known as publicly traded funds, *closed-end funds* make a one-time offering of new shares. This is how they raise the money to be invested in the common portfolio. Once the portfolio is assembled, the fund manages it on a continuing basis, striving to achieve the investment objective(s) of the fund. The fund shares trade in the open market, either on a stock exchange or over-the-counter. Through this secondary market, investors who did not purchase shares on the initial offering can still buy into the fund, and current owners can dispose of their shares. After the initial offering, the fund itself is no longer involved in the trading of the shares of the fund. Management's job is to manage the shares and bonds *owned* by the fund, the fund's portfolio. The capitalization of a closed-end fund can be quite complex and may consist of several different classes of stock and other securities. The open-market prices of closed-end fund shares are rarely equal to their net asset value. Some closed-end funds trade higher than NAV (at a premium), while most trade at per-share prices lower than NAV (at a discount).

OPEN-END FUNDS

Open-end funds are more popularly known as *mutual funds*. There are several thousands of these companies, with an almost limitless variety of investment objectives. Unlike closed-end funds, mutual funds usually issue only a single class of voting common stock. They can invest in almost anything—stocks, bonds, options—but they only *issue* common stock. Mutual funds continuously offer new shares, standing ready to issue additional fund shares at all times in response to orders from the public.

Mutual funds also redeem outstanding shares from shareholders. In the strictest sense, you do not sell mutual fund shares, but rather you *redeem* them. The effect is the same, but the fund retires the shares you redeem, which results in fewer fund shares outstanding. While the mutual fund has a simple capitalization—common shares only—the number of such common shares outstanding constantly changes. Outstanding shares are reduced by redemptions, but are increased as people continue to purchase additional shares of the fund. Unlike the closed-end fund that makes only a one-time offering, the open-end (mutual) fund is a perennial new issue. It is this simple but ever-changing capitalization that distinguishes the open-end fund from the closed-end fund.

QUOTATIONS

Closed-end funds may be traded on an exchange (listed) or OTC (over-the-counter or unlisted). The bid and asked prices for closed-end funds are set by the investing public (supply and demand) and may be higher or lower than the funds' actual net asset values. A typical quotation might read

"21.15–21.20." The bid (21.15) is the highest price at which anyone is willing to buy shares of the closed-end fund, while the offer (21.20) is the lowest price at which anyone is willing to sell. The fund's actual NAV might be higher or lower than the quoted prices.

The NAVs of open-end funds (mutual funds) are also expressed in dollars and cents, but mutual funds are never listed on an exchange and only trade OTC. [This text will not cover Exchange Traded Funds (ETFs), which are listed and may be bought and sold throughout the trading day. They are index-based investment products.] A typical mutual fund quotation might read "10.24–11.01." Although referred to as the "bid" and "asked" prices, the first value shown ($10.24) is actually the fund's net asset value (NAV), while the second figure ($11.01) is the cost of purchasing a share of the fund. The difference between the two figures, $0.77 ($11.01-$10.24), is the fund's sales charge, or *load*.

Investment Companies

	Closed-End Funds	Open-End Funds
Trade On	Exchanges or OTC	OTC
Pricing	Bid / Ask	NAV / Offer Price
	Difference = Spread	Difference = Load
Redemption	Shares are not redeemed, but are sold to another buyer.	Shares are redeemed by fund and outstanding shares are reduced by that amount.
Capitalization	May be complex.	Simple

LOAD FUNDS VERSUS NO-LOAD FUNDS

No-load funds do not levy an up-front sales charge, or load. Some no-load funds levy a charge if their shares are redeemed fairly soon after they are purchased. These *back-end loads* or *contingent deferred sales charges* may be relatively high if the funds are redeemed fairly soon after they are purchased, but are usually reduced over time.

Many mutual funds are no-load funds. Their quotations might read: "13.22–NL" or: "14.07–14.07." Both quotations convey essentially the same information and indicate a mutual fund that does not levy a sales charge. The "NL" used as the asked price in the first quotation stands for "no load" and shows that the fund can be both bought and sold (redeemed) at the same price. The second quotation example (14.07–14.07) also indicates a no-load fund.

Loaded funds can take as much as 8.5% of the amount invested, but relatively few funds do so. Most loaded funds levy commission charges averaging about 5%.

BREAKPOINTS

Most loaded mutual funds offer *breakpoints*, which are reduced sales charges for large purchases. For example, if the load on Marobeth Fund is ordinarily 6%, such a charge might apply only to purchases of less than $10,000 worth of fund shares. The sales charge might be reduced to 5% for bulk purchases between $10,000 and $25,000 and further reduced to 4% for purchases between $25,000 and $50,000. The different amounts one must buy to obtain these reduced loads are known as breakpoints. The scale of such reduced loads differs from fund to fund. You must consult each loaded fund's prospectus for details.

RIGHT OF ACCUMULATION

Most loaded funds also offer another method of reducing the sales charge, called the *right of accumulation*. Refer to the pricing structure in the paragraph about breakpoints. We will assume that Kristen Cartlidge has been making many small, regular purchases of Marobeth Fund at regular time intervals (this is known as *dollar cost averaging*, a popular strategy). Kristen has been buying $1,000 of Marobeth Fund each month for the past nine months. These purchases were all made at the 6% sales charge level because they did not qualify for the $10,000 breakpoint. Ms. Cartlidge's next purchase will bring her purchases to date to the $10,000 level, but on this particular $1,000 investment she will be charged only the 5% rate. The lower rate will also apply to any other purchases until she reaches the $25,000 level, after which Kristen will be charged the 4% rate.

LETTER OF INTENT

Sometimes investors would like to invest an amount in a load mutual fund at a breakpoint to lower the sales charge, but they are hesitant to make such a large purchase at one time for fear of buying at a market high. Many funds offer a way to do both; spread out smaller purchases over time and still take advantage of a reduced sales charge. To accomplish this, investors sign a *letter of intent* that allows them to take up to 13 months to buy enough shares, a little at a time, to qualify for a breakpoint. Even though the individual purchases would not qualify for the reduced sales charge, so long as the total purchases over the 13-month period meet the breakpoint, each purchase is charged only the lower fee. Refer to the sales charges we have described for Marobeth Fund: Under a $10,000 letter of intent, an investor can spread out her fund purchases over 13 months (about $800 per month, for instance) and be charged only the 5% sales load for each purchase.

FORWARD PRICING

Mutual funds figure their net asset values as of 4 p.m. Eastern time each business day, using the market prices in effect at the time the New York Stock Exchange closes. All buy and sell orders entered before 4 p.m. on a day the New York Stock Exchange is open are executed at that same day's 4 p.m. closing prices. The buys are executed at the funds' offer price, and the sells (redemptions) are executed at the funds' bid (NAV) price.

Orders entered after 4 p.m. Eastern time are executed at the *following* day's closing quotations. This system of receiving and paying the next quotations to be calculated after orders are entered is known as *forward pricing*.

PROSPECTUS REQUIREMENTS

A mutual fund is a perennial new issue. New shares are issued by the fund in response to customers' orders to buy, and outstanding shares are canceled in response to customers' requests for redemption. Since every purchase of a mutual fund is a new issue, it is covered by the Securities Act of 1933, the "full disclosure" act. To ensure that clients purchasing a mutual fund have full information about it, they must receive a current prospectus no later than the time when they receive their confirmation of purchase. They must also receive a new prospectus, so long as they own the fund, each time a revised prospectus is issued. Fund shareholders also receive regular interim reports from any mutual funds that they own.

REINVESTING DIVIDENDS AND CAPITAL GAINS

Each mutual fund owner is entitled to receive his or her proportionate share of any dividends, interest, and capital gains earned by the fund. The vast majority of fund investors choose to have the fund automatically reinvest such distributions in additional shares of the fund. This has a similar compounding effect to earning interest in a savings account and allowing it to remain in the account rather than withdrawing it, so as to earn "interest on interest." Many fund investors reinvest all distributions during their working years, and then in retirement switch to a system whereby the dividends and interest, and sometimes the capital gains as well, are paid to them in cash instead of being reinvested.

It is very important to be aware that a fund shareholder is responsible for taxes on any distributions—dividends, interest, and capital gains— whether reinvested in additional shares or received in cash.

MUTUAL FUND OBJECTIVES

Investors must be aware that there is no such thing as the "best" mutual fund among the many thousands of different funds from which to choose. Every fund has a stated investment objective, and investors should choose funds that have the same investment objective as they (the investors) do. While there are more than 40 different objectives, we discuss only a few general ones: preservation of capital, income, and growth. These broadly cover the range from very safe investment vehicles to very speculative choices.

Preservation of Capital   Investors with this objective should limit their choices to the safest vehicles, possibly including money market funds (investing only in short-term debt instruments), U.S. government bond funds, and conservative corporate or municipal bond funds holding only highly rated bonds.

Income   Investors interested in seeking a second source of income would gravitate toward the many income funds available. These do not afford the same degree of safety as the preservation of capital vehicles, but that is to be expected if one wants to enjoy generous income. You have to expose yourself to a certain degree of risk to gain additional income. No investment combines both a high degree of safety and generous income. Income funds might include the same general types of securities as some of the preservation of capital funds, but they would probably hold corporate or municipal bonds of lesser quality and, consequently, higher yield.

Growth   Those seeking growth are ordinarily not interested primarily in income. They are after capital gains and are willing to take on a fair degree of risk in pursuit of that objective. There are relatively conservative growth funds and more aggressive ones, to suit the many different degrees of risk that investors might be willing to assume. Such funds ordinarily invest in stocks rather than bonds, and might specialize in small-cap or mid-cap stocks, newer issues, foreign stocks, short positions, or options.

Risk / Return

Lower Risk **Lower Return**		**Higher Risk** **Higher Return**
Preservation of Capital	**Income**	**Growth**
Money Market Funds	High-Yield Bond Funds	Equity and International or
Government Bond Funds	Preferred Stock Funds	Global Funds
Conservative Corporate or		
Municipal Bond Funds		

SUMMARY

The most popular type of investment company in the United States is the mutual fund. There are currently more than 6,000 of them, designed to meet a great variety of investment objectives ranging from the most conservative to the most speculative. They afford diversification, convenience, and professional management, and are particularly well suited to dollar cost averaging, a system of making regular investments at regular time intervals, without regard to the level of the market. Most mutual funds are no-load; those that are loaded may impose a sales charge of as much as 8.5% of the amount invested. Their net asset values are calculated every business day at 4 p.m. New York time, and orders to buy and sell are executed at the next prices established after such orders are received.

MULTIPLE-CHOICE QUIZ

1. What would be the total cost of 100 shares of XYZ Fund if it were quoted at 12.68–13.49 at the 4 p.m. pricing after the receipt of the buy order?
   a. $ 1,268.00
   b. $ 1,308.50
   c. $ 1,349.00
   d. cannot be determined from the information presented

2. Which of the following are considered advantages of investing in mutual funds?
   I   diversification
   II ability to reinvest dividends without paying tax
   III professional management
   IV convenience
   a. I and III only
   b. II and IV only
   c. I, III, and IV only
   d. I, II, III, and IV

3. A mutual fund's net asset value is equal to its:
   a. par value
   b. net liability price
   c. liquidating value
   d. original offering price

4. A loaded mutual fund's maximum sales charge may be no greater than what percent of the amount invested?
   a. 4.25
   b. 5.5
   c. 6.25
   d. 8.5

5. A client interested in making the value of investments increase over time and willing to assume a fair degree of risk in order to achieve this would most probably choose a(an):
   a. preservation of capital fund
   b. money market fund
   c. income fund
   d. growth fund

PRACTICE EXERCISES

1. Which of the following investment companies is (are) publicly traded?

	Net Asset Value	Offer Price
a.	$12.12	$14.50
b.	$32.49	$31.75
c.	$26.50	$31.25
d.	$41.74	$40.00

2. A friend of yours is considering a long-term investment plan through the purchase of mutual funds in a non-IRA account. She will automatically reinvest all distributions from her mutual fund holdings, both dividends and capital gains, rather than taking them in cash. Must she pay taxes on such distributions, or may they be deferred until she eventually sells the additional fund shares obtained through reinvestment?

3. An investor wants to purchase $50,000 of a growth mutual fund to take advantage of the 4% sales charge on purchases of that amount, but is reluctant to do so because she fears that she might be purchasing at a market high. She is tempted to spread out her purchases over the next year, even though such purchases would be for less than $10,000 each and as such would be subject to an 8.5% load. What might she consider?

For questions 4 to 6, calculate all offering prices to the nearest cent. Calculate the percent sales charge to *two* decimal places. Calculate the number of shares to *three* decimal places.

4. Zenobia Fund has a net asset value of $12.27 and levies the legal maximum sales charge for a voluntary plan. What is the fund's offering price?

5. Aratusa Fund is quoted 14.44 – 15.61. What is the fund's maximum sales charge expressed in the usual industry manner?

6. Panoceanic Fund has a net asset value of $9.93 and levies a sales charge (expressed as a percentage of the offering price) of 8% for purchases of up to $10,000, 6% for purchases between $10,000 and $25,000, and 5% for purchases over $25,000. How many shares would be purchased by a client ordering $35,000 worth of the fund?

MULTIPLE-CHOICE ANSWERS AND EXPLANATIONS

1. **c.** Buy orders are executed at the offering price calculated at 4 p.m. after the receipt of the order. The buy would be executed at the offering price shown—$13.49—and 100 shares would cost a total of $1,349.00.

2. **c.** It is not possible to immediately reinvest mutual fund dividends and thus escape tax. The tax must be paid whether the distributions are reinvested or taken in cash.

3. **c.** A mutual fund's net asset value (NAV) is the actual value of a fund share. It is calculated by adding together all the fund's assets, subtracting its liabilities, and dividing by the number of mutual fund shares outstanding. It is the fund's liquidating value, the amount each fund share would be entitled to if the fund were to be liquidated.

4. **d.** The maximum is 8.5%. Very few funds charge this amount, however. Most of the newer funds are no-load or low-load. Some funds levy a charge not when you purchase the fund, but at the time you redeem it; such funds are known as back-end load funds. The back-end load is normally reduced over time, so that if the fund is held long enough there is little or no charge when redeeming.

5. **d.** That's the classic definition of a growth fund. Remember that there are many different types of growth funds—some for those willing to accept only a relatively small risk, and others for those willing and able to assume a large risk in the hope of reaping large rewards.

ANSWERS TO PRACTICE EXERCISES

1. All are publicly traded.

   All the investment companies listed are publicly traded or closed-end funds. Choices a and c are being offered at premiums of about 20% above their net asset values. Open-end funds (mutual funds) can never trade at a premium over their NAVs of more than about 9%. Choices b and d are being offered at discounts to their NAVs. Only closed-end funds can be so traded; mutual funds can never trade at a discount.

2. Taxes must be paid in the year of the distributions, whether taken in cash or automatically reinvested.

   This is an important point. While it may pose a small financial hardship to pay taxes when there is no offsetting flow of cash, it might be considered a form of "forced savings." The amounts reinvested are, in effect, additional purchases, and add to the investor's cost of the holding. Thus, when the shares are ultimately sold, they have a higher cost basis than the total of the client's direct cash contributions.

3. She should consider signing a letter of intent.

   Almost all load funds offer such an option. She could sign a $50,000 letter of intent and purchase her shares in monthly amounts of approximately $4,200 over the following year. Each such purchase, even though in the 8.5% sales bracket, would be processed with only the 4% sales charge normally applicable to purchases of $50,000 or more. She will have accomplished her goal of spreading out her purchases but will have avoided the high sales charges.

4. $13.41

   The legal maximum charge for a noncontractual plan is 8.50% of the offering price.

   $$\text{Offer Price} = \frac{\text{Net Asset Value}}{100\% - \text{Sales Charge }\%}$$

   $$\text{Offer Price} = \frac{\$12.27}{100\% - 8.50\%}$$

   $$\text{Offer Price} = \frac{\$12.27}{.915} = \$13.41$$

5. 7.5%

    $15.61 − $14.44 = $1.17 (the sales charge)

    $$\frac{\$1.17}{\$15.61} = 7.50\%$$

6. 3349.282 shares

    The 5% sales charge applies to the entire purchase.

    $$\frac{\$9.93}{100\% - 5\%} = \frac{\$9.93}{.95} = \$10.45 \text{ offer price}$$

    $$\frac{\$35,000}{\$10.45} = 3349.282 \text{ shares}$$

Call Option Basics

STOCK OPTIONS

Call options give their owners the right to buy stock at a set price. While call option holders have this right, they do not have any obligations. They *may* exercise the option, but they are not forced to do so. Think of it as buying a ticket to a concert; the ticket holder may attend the concert, but is not forced to do so. Call options give their owners the right to *buy* stock, while *put options* (described in Chapter 14) give their owners the right to *sell* stock. Our discussion covers only listed stock options that are currently traded on five different exchanges: the Chicago Board Options Exchange (CBOE), the American Stock Exchange, the Philadelphia Stock Exchange, the International Securities Exchange, and the Pacific Stock Exchange.

HOW OPTIONS ARE DESCRIBED

Most corporations have only a single class of outstanding common stock, so normally we have only to state "100 shares of YAC" and the presumption is that we are referring to 100 shares of YAC common stock. If YAC has preferred stock outstanding as well, we cannot assume that it has issued only one class of preferred, as many corporations issue several such fixed-income equity securities (described in detail in Chapter 4). We must identify the particular preferred we are referring to by enhancing the stock's description, such as "YAC 8% preferred" or "YAC $2.40 preferred." We also have to identify particular bonds (there may be many bonds of the same issuer outstanding at one time), usually by including the interest (coupon) rate and year of maturity as part of the description, such as "YAC 9s of '08," or "YAC $10^1/_2$s of '20."

Singling out a particular stock option from among the many options that may be traded on that same stock is slightly more complicated. In addition to the name of the stock that it can be used to buy or sell, an option's description also includes three other elements: the *strike price*, the *month of expiration*, and the *type* of option.

For example, let's examine "1 YAC April 40 call." This particular option gives its owner the right to buy 100 shares of YAC common stock at $40 per share until late next April. Remember the rights and warrants discussed in Chapter 3? Call options are similar in that they also confer the right to buy common stock. We will explain each element of the option's description, in turn.

1 *YAC April 40 call*—The "1" indicates that this is 1 call, which conveys the right to buy *100 shares* of stock. Every call option carries the right to buy 100 shares of stock. Two calls permit the purchase of 200 shares, 10 calls cover 1,000 shares, and so on.

1 **YAC** *April 40 call*—YAC common stock is the *underlying security*, the stock that the call owner can purchase. There are options outstanding on hundreds of different stocks. In addition to YAC 40 calls, there may also be ABC 40 calls, XYX 40 calls, etc.

1 YAC **April** *40 call*—The *expiration month* is next April. There will be other YAC options trading that expire in other months, such as YAC May 40 calls or YAC August 40 calls. Unlike rights, which usually expire in a month or less after they are issued, stock options can have exercise periods of as long as several years.

1 YAC April **40** *call*—Here, 40 is the *strike price*, also known as the *striking* or *exercise price*. There will be other YAC April call options with other strike prices, usually at 5-point intervals, such as YAC April 35 calls or YAC April 45 calls.

1 YAC April 40 **call**—This is the *type* of option (a call), which permits its owner to *buy* stock. It is very different from a YAC April 40 put.

OPTION PREMIUMS

The market price of an option, set by supply and demand, is known as its *premium*. If the YAC option we have been discussing is trading at a premium of 2.50, it has a market value of $250, not $2.50! Each option covers 100 shares of stock, and an option's price must be multiplied by 100 to arrive at its actual dollar value. An option quoted at 3.00 has a market value of $300, and two options trading at 4.50 have a dollar value of $900.

OPTIONS FOR LEVERAGE

A person owning a YAC April 40 call has the right to buy 100 shares of YAC common stock, until late April, at $40 per share—a fixed price. Why would an investor want to buy this option? She is bullish on YAC and expects it to rise in price. Let's compare how the investor might attempt to profit from what she perceives as a coming upswing in the price of YAC common stock from 40 to 52. She has about $4,000 to invest. We will first look at the more conventional approaches—buying the stock in a cash account, then in a margin account—and then explore the use of call options.

The most traditional approach is for the investor to purchase 100 shares of YAC in a cash account. If she did so, her cost would be $4,000 (100 shares @ 40.00). If she then sold the stock after it rose to 52 ($5,200) her profit would be $1,200, which is a 30% gain on her original investment. Her potential profit was unlimited (theoretically, there is no limit to how high YAC could have gone in price), and her maximum possible loss (her risk) was $4,000, had YAC gone bankrupt.

A second approach is for the investor to use a margin account and buy 200 shares of YAC for the same $4,000. If the stock moved to 52.00, she would have a profit of $2,400, a 60% gain on her original investment. Please keep in mind that she would have to pay interest charges on her margin account's debit balance and, if YAC went down instead of up, she would lose twice as much on the margin transaction as she would on a cash transaction. You can make twice as much in a margin account—or lose twice as much! Her profit potential is again unlimited, but she could lose her entire investment of $4,000. (Margin trading is discussed in Chapter 19.)

Here's a third approach: buying a call option. If an April YAC call option with a strike price of $40 is selling for 3.00 ($300), she might buy one call at that price. She now has the right to buy 100 shares of YAC at $40 per share at any time until the option expires late next April. If, during the option's life, YAC rose in price to 52.00, she could exercise her option (buying 100 YAC at $40 per share) and then immediately sell the 100 shares at the higher market price, 52.00. Her overall gain would be $900 (the sale for $5,200 less the exercise price of $4,000 and the $300 cost of the option), a 300% profit! Note that her maximum loss can only be $300, the cost of the option. This is an important consideration. When you *buy* an option you can lose only the premium (the cost of the option itself).

This illustrates one of the principal reasons certain investors buy calls when they are bullish on a stock, rather than purchasing the stock outright; buying calls provides *leverage*. Call buyers hope to realize a great deal of profit from a relatively small investment, and their possibility of loss is limited to that same small investment.

Note: **In these illustrations, as in all the other examples in this book, we have not taken into account the commissions and taxes that might have to be paid by the option trader. Such costs can be considerable, and it is important to understand that the actual profits shown will be smaller—and the losses greater—than the figures we have indicated.**

THE INTRINSIC VALUE OF STOCK OPTIONS

While YAC common stock is trading at 40.00, all YAC 40 call options are said to be *at-the-money*. This indicates that there would be no profit or loss if the option were exercised and the underlying shares were immediately sold. It does not make sense to go through the trouble of exercising (buying) at 40 and then selling at 40 for no gain. This is true for all options when their strike prices are the same as the current market prices for the underlying stocks. An at-the-money option has no *intrinsic* (built-in) value.

When a call option's strike price is higher than the underlying stock's current market price, the option is said to be *out-of-the-money*. A 55 call would have no intrinsic value if the underlying stock was trading at 52.00 in the open market. It would make no sense to exercise (buy) at 55.00 and then sell at 52.00, as that would result in an outright loss. Out-of-the-money options, like at-the-money options, have no intrinsic value.

If a call option's strike price is lower than the underlying stock's current market price, the option is said to be *in-the-money*. If, for instance, a stock were trading at 48.00, a call option on that stock with a strike price of 45 (a 45 call) would be worth at least 3. The call would allow the purchase (exercise) of stock at 45.00 per share, and the shares could be sold immediately thereafter at 48.00 per share. This option has an intrinsic value of 3. All in-the-money options have intrinsic value.

THE TIME VALUE OF STOCK OPTIONS

When an option's price—its premium—exceeds its intrinsic value (as is almost always the case), the option is said to have *time value*. When the option is at-the-money or out-of-the-money (and thus has no intrinsic value), the entire premium is time value. When the option is in-the-money, the amount by which its price (the premium) exceeds its intrinsic value is time value.

Examples

1. A 60 call is priced at 4.00 while the underlying stock is trading in the open market at 60.00. The option is at-the-money and has no intrinsic value. The option's premium, 4.00, is its time value. In this instance the entire premium consists of time value.

2. An 80 call is priced at 2.00 while the underlying stock is trading in the open market at 79.00. The option is out-of-the-money and has no intrinsic value. The option's premium, 2.00, is its time value. Here again, the entire premium consists of time value.

3. A 70 call is priced at 7.00 while the underlying stock is trading in the open market at 74.00. The option is 4 points in-the-money and thus has an intrinsic value of 4. Since the price of the option is 7.00, it exceeds the option's intrinsic value by 3 points. The option's time value is 3. In this situation, the option's price (7.00) consists of both intrinsic value (4) and time value (3).

WASTING ASSETS

Options are classified as *wasting assets*. This reflects the fact that stock options, as they near expiration, lose more and more of their time value. It make sense, because while investors are willing to pay extra (time value) for an option when there is a lot of time left before expiration, as the option nears expiration there is less and less time for the underlying stock to move in the right direction. Time value is just that—options with a long time before expiration have relatively high time value, but options approaching expiration have less and less time value. Here's an example:

An XYZ 70 call expiring in eight months might be selling at 6.00 when the underlying stock is trading at 69.00. The option is out-of-the-money and has no intrinsic value. The price of the option consists only of time value. The call buyer might reason, "Even though the option is out-of-the-money right now, I think that during the next six months XYZ will rise to about 85.00. If it does, I can exercise the option at 70.00, sell the stock at 85.00, and make $900 profit ($8,500 sale – $7,000 exercise price and the $600 cost of the option). I'll take a chance and buy the option." What if, instead of going up, XYZ is still at 69.00 four months later when the option is halfway to expiration? Would that same investor still be willing to pay 6.00 for the option now that it has a shorter life? At least in theory, the option would now be trading lower, probably at 3.00 or less. Let's suppose that XYZ never moves from a price of 69.00, and it's still there when the option has only a day or so of life. What kind of time value would people be willing to pay for an out-of-the-money option that has only a few days to run? That's right, virtually nothing.

HOW CALL OPTIONS ARE CREATED

It takes both a seller and a buyer to create an option. Unless someone agrees to sell (write) an RFW July 50 call, you cannot buy one. Similarly, unless someone agrees to buy it, you cannot write (sell) a CER April 65 call.

There are stock options on virtually all widely traded stocks. Interestingly, the boards of directors of the underlying stocks have no control over whether publicly traded (listed) options on their securities will exist at all, what their strike prices and expiration months will be, or where they will be traded. Call options are created by willing buyers and sellers—those who have the right to buy the underlying stock (the owners of the call) and others who have the obligation to sell the underlying stock to the call owner if exercised (the writers of the call). For every buyer of a call option, there has to be a seller. The buyer (who is said to be *long* the call option) and the seller (also known as the *writer* of the option) have opposite opinions as to the future price movement of the underlying stock.

The buyer, long the option, is bullish and thinks the stock will go up in price. After all, she has the right to buy the stock at a fixed price, so she hopes the stock will go well above the exercise price, enabling her to buy the stock at the fixed price and sell the stock at the higher market price. For the call option buyer, the higher the stock goes, the better. The call buyer has, at least in theory, an unlimited profit potential, while her loss can be no greater than the price she pays for the call (the premium). The call buyer paid a premium for the right to buy stock, but is under no obligation to do so.

The seller, short the option, is bearish and thinks the stock will go down in price. When he sells the option he is saying, in effect, "Hey, Ms. Option Buyer, you think the stock will go up. I think you're wrong, so let's bet on it. If you pay me the premium, I'll give you the right to buy the stock from me, at the strike price, at any time you want during the life of the option. That's the deal—you pay me the premium and I'll give you the right to buy stock at the strike price. I'll assume the obligation to sell you that stock if and when you exercise."

Options are a *zero-sum* game. By this we mean that the amount the buyer of the option makes as a profit will be the loss suffered by the seller of the option, and any loss suffered by the option buyer represents that same amount of profit for the option seller. Consider this example:

A bullish speculator pays 2.00 for an NFW May 35 call. NFW is trading at 35.00, so the call is at-the-money and has no intrinsic value. The seller of the option (the writer) receives the $200 premium. We will assume that the seller is not long any NFW stock, so he is called a *naked* or *uncovered* writer. Before the option expires, NFW has risen in price to 41.00 and the option buyer exercises by buying stock from the option writer at 35.00. The option writer must go into the open market and buy NFW stock at 41.00 so he can sell it to the option buyer at the agreed-upon strike price of 35. The writer thus has to buy stock at 41.00 in the open market and sell it to the call buyer at 35.00. He suffers a $600 loss on this buy/sell transaction, but loses only $400 overall because he originally received a $200 premium when he wrote (sold) the option.

Now let's look at the profit for the option buyer: She paid $200 for the option and then made $600 on the buy/sell transaction (she exercised at 35 and immediately sold the stock in the open market at 41), for an overall profit of $400. The amount the option buyer makes equals the amount the option seller loses.

Now let's change the situation. What if, during the life of the option, NFW had never risen above 35 a share? The option buyer would not have exercised and the option would have expired worthless. The option buyer would have lost the entire premium of $200, and the option seller would have kept the entire premium—the same $200. Again, what the option buyer loses, the option seller makes. That's why it's called a zero-sum game.

SUMMARY

Call options confer upon their owners the right to buy stock at a set price for the life of the option. The owner of the option (said to be long the option) paid a premium—the option's price—for this right. The most he can lose is the premium he paid. He is bullish and wishes the underlying stock to go well above the strike price so he can either exercise at the strike price and sell the stock thus acquired at the higher market price, or simply sell the call option for more than he paid for it.

The writers (sellers) of call options receive a premium and are under an obligation to sell stock to the option buyer if exercised. The writer's profit is limited to the amounts he received for the premium. A call writer is bearish and does not expect the market price of the underlying stock to rise. Once a call option is purchased it may be sold at a later time, may be used (exercised), or might simply expire.

MULTIPLE-CHOICE QUIZ

1. What is the intrinsic value (if any) of an XYZ August 55 call trading at 3.50 when the underlying stock is selling at 54.00?

   a. 0

   b. 1.00

   c. 2.50

   d. 3.50

2. What is the time value (if any) of the option described in question 1?

   a. 0

   b. 1.00

   c. 2.50

   d. 3.50

3. What is the profit potential for the buyer of an ABC November 45 call if he pays 3.00 for the option?

   a. $ 300

   b. $ 420

   c. $ 480

   d. unlimited

4. What is the maximum loss potential for the buyer of the option described in question 3?

   a. $ 300

   b. $ 420

   c. $ 480

   d. unlimited

5. What would be the total cost for five YAC January 20 calls trading at 4.00?

   a. $ 20

   b. $ 200

   c. $ 2,000

   d. $ 20,000

PRACTICE EXERCISES

An XYZ April 50 call has a premium of 1.50 while the underlying stock is trading at 49.00.

1. Is the option in-the-money, out-of-the-money, or at-the-money?

2. What is the option's intrinsic value, if any?

3. What is the option's time value, if any?

4. What is the maximum profit potential for a *buyer* of this option?

5. What is the maximum loss potential for a *buyer* of this option?

6. What is the maximum profit potential for the *writer* of this option?

7. What is the maximum loss potential for the *writer* of this option?

8. Excluding commissions, what would be the total dollar cost for 10 of these options?

MULTIPLE-CHOICE ANSWERS AND EXPLANATIONS

1. **a.** The option has no intrinsic value. It is out-of-the-money by 1 point. There would be no profit—in fact, there would be a 1-point loss—in exercising the call at a strike price of 55 when the underlying stock was trading at 54.00.

2. **d.** Since there is no intrinsic value, then the price of the option—the premium—consists only of time value. Had the market price of the underlying stock been 56.00, then the option would have been in-the-money by 1 point. This in-the-money value would have been its intrinsic value and the option's price of 3.50 would then have consisted of two elements, intrinsic value of 1 point and time value of 2.5 points.

3. **d.** Long call options have an unlimited profit potential. Long call positions, like all long stock positions, have no "top" profit limit because there is no limit to how high a stock might rise in price. This is one of the advantages of buying calls rather than purchasing stock outright: You have the opportunity to make a relatively large profit on a relatively modest investment.

4. **a.** All the call buyer can lose is the premium paid. At worst, the option will expire worthless. The owner of the option has the right to do something, but has no obligation to do anything. Limiting your potential loss to only the premium you paid is another advantage of buying calls.

5. **c.** A single call priced at 4.00 would cost $400 (100 × 4.00). The total cost of five calls at 4.00 is $2,000.

ANSWERS TO PRACTICE EXERCISES

1. The option is out-of-the-money.

   There would be no advantage to exercising a call (buying) at 50.00 when the underlying stock is trading at less than that price.

2. The option has no intrinsic value.

   At-the-money and out-of-the-money options have no intrinsic value; only in-the-money options have intrinsic value.

3. The option's time value is 1.50 points.

   Since there is no intrinsic value, the option's premium consists only of time value.

4. Unlimited

   At least in theory, there is no limit to how high the underlying stock might rise.

5. $150

   The purchaser of an option can lose only the amount paid for the option (the premium). An option's purchaser has the right to do something, but is under no obligation to do anything.

6. $150

   That's as good as it can get for the option writer. He can keep the premium he received when he wrote the option. Note that the option buyer's maximum *loss* potential is the same as the option writer's *profit* potential.

7. Unlimited

   Refer to the explanation for answer 4. Since options are a zero-sum game, the option buyer's maximum profit potential is the same as the option writer's maximum loss potential.

8. $1,500

   One option trading at 1.50 costs $150. Ten such options cost a total of $1,500.

CHAPTER 13

Call Option Strategies

WHAT ULTIMATELY HAPPENS TO AN OPTION?

There are three possible endings for an option owned (or written) by an investor: The option might be exercised, the option might expire, or the option might be traded in the open market. Let's examine all three possibilities, showing the consequences for both the buyer and the seller of the option in each instance. In all three cases we will assume that, sometime during May, Mr. Bull bought an at-the-money IBM July 105 call from Mr. Bear for 12.00. Mr. Bear was not long any IBM stock at the time he sold (wrote) the call, so he was a naked (uncovered) writer. The premium of $1,200 was paid by Mr. Bull to Mr. Bear. Mr. Bull then had the right to buy 100 shares of IBM at 105 per share, if he chose to do so, until late in the month of July. Mr. Bear had an obligation to sell 100 shares of IBM to Mr. Bull if he was asked to do so (if he were exercised) at any time before the option expired in late July.

The Three Scenarios

1. *The option is exercised.* Let us assume that during June, IBM stock had a dramatic rise in price to 131 and Mr. Bull exercised his call option. He would exercise by buying 100 IBM at 105 from Mr. Bear, paying him $10,500. He would then sell the shares in the open market at 131, for $13,100. Mr. Bull paid $1,200 for the option and then made $2,600 by exercising (buying) for $10,500 and selling for $13,100. He thus had a net profit of $1,400 on his investment of only $1,200.

Mr. Bear, who was uncovered, has to buy IBM in the marketplace at its current price of 131 for $13,100 and must sell it to Mr. Bull at the strike price of 105 ($10,500). He loses $2,600 on the trade, but this loss is partly offset by the $1,200 premium he received when he originally sold the option to Mr. Bull. Mr. Bear thus has an overall loss of $1,400. Note that Mr. Bear's loss of $1,400 is equal to Mr. Bull's profit of $1,400.

2. *The option expires.* Mr. Bear was right all along and, instead of going up in price, IBM stayed at or below 105 through the end of July. It will do Mr. Bull no good to exercise an at-the-money or out-of-the-money option. He wouldn't exercise the call at 105 a share unless he were able to sell the shares he would receive at a higher price in the open market. In this case, Mr. Bull simply loses his bet and the option expires in late July. Mr. Bull is out the entire premium of $1,200 (his loss), and Mr. Bear retains the entire premium of $1,200 (his profit). Again, what Mr. Bull loses, Mr. Bear gains.

3. *The option is traded.* Keep in mind that owners and writers of options are not necessarily locked into their positions until expiration date. There is a way they can give up their rights—or discharge their obligations—while the option is still in force. An option owner can simply sell the option in the open market at any time. He is long the option and can go flat simply by selling it. Once he sells, of course, he no longer has the right to exercise. In the same manner, at any time before he is exercised, a writer who is short the option can buy the same type of option in the open market to offset the position. Here again, he would go flat and thus be rid of his obligation to honor an exercise.

The premium on the July IBM option will fluctuate during its life. It will track the price of IBM, going up and down as IBM stock rises and falls. (An option is a *derivative security* because its market price is "derived" from the price of another security, in this case, IBM common stock.) If the option were subsequently to trade at 14.00, the option buyer could sell at that price and have a $200 profit (bought for $1,200, sold for $1,400). If, instead, he decided to sell when the option was trading at 3.00, he would have a loss of $900 (bought for $1,200, sold for $300). Similarly, the option writer can buy an offsetting call at any time before he is exercised, at either a profit or a loss, and thus be rid of his obligation. If the writer buys back (covers) the option at 15.00, he will have a loss of $300 (sold for $1,200, bought for $1,500). If he covers at 4.00, he will have a profit of $800 (sold for $1,200, bought for $400).

BREAKEVEN PRICES FOR CALL BUYERS AND WRITERS

Claudette Morgan buys an XYZ 45 call for 3.50. When her option expires, what market price for XYZ will allow her to break even, neither making or losing money on her investment? Ms. Morgan will break even if XYZ is at 48.50 when the option expires. At 48.50, the 45 call option will be in-the-money by 3.50 points and its intrinsic value will be 3.50. Ms. Morgan could exercise at 45 and immediately sell XYZ for 48.50, which would give her a

3.50 point trading profit, exactly offsetting her call option's purchase price. She would thus break even on the transactions.

How about the writer of the option Claudette purchased? Mrs. Roberta Cartlidge wrote the 45 call option naked. Roberta received the $350 premium and has the same breakeven point (48.50) as Claudette. If Mrs. Cartlidge is exercised at 45, she must go into the open market to buy 100 XYZ at 48.50 and sell it to Ms. Morgan at 45. This trading loss of $350 is exactly balanced by the $350 premium she received when she wrote the option.

Since options are a zero-sum game, any profit for the buyer is the same as the loss for the seller, any loss for the buyer is the same as the profit for the seller, and both buyer and seller have the same breakeven point.

CALL OPTIONS AS A HEDGE

While trading options is normally considered a speculative activity, there are many other uses for options, including *hedging*. Call options may be bought as a form of insurance that can either protect a short position against a catastrophic loss or protect an already-established profit on a short position. We will illustrate each of these concepts.

Note that, in theory, there is no limit to how much a speculator might lose on a short sale. After all, he has borrowed stock to deliver against his short sale, and someday must buy back shares to "cover" the transaction so that he can return the borrowed shares. There is no way of telling what price he will eventually have to pay to buy the shares because there is, at least in theory, no limit to how high a stock can go in price. The short seller is facing a huge potential loss. How can he protect himself? By buying a call! Here's how it works.

Ralph Chirico is bearish on DEF and thinks it will decline dramatically in price from its present trading level of 97 per share. He shorts 100 shares at 97, hoping to be able to buy it back later (to cover) at a much lower price. His maximum potential profit is $9,700, as he wants the stock to go down in price and the lowest price it can sink to is zero. It may be far-fetched but, at least in theory, DEF could go bankrupt and Mr. Chirico could then buy back (cover) the 100 shares for nothing. Having sold short for $9,700 and having bought back (covered) at zero, his profit would be $9,700. But how much might he lose if the stock goes up instead of down? There's no limit to Ralph's potential loss because there is no limit to how high DEF might go. Ralph does not like to be in a position with a definite limit to how much he can make but no limit to how much he might lose.

Here's how Ralph can protect himself, at least to some extent. After shorting DEF at 97, he also purchases an out-of-the-money DEF 100 call for 4.00. He has bought the call not because he is bullish, but as a form of insurance against DEF going way up in price and causing him to lose a large amount on his short position. He hopes that DEF will go down and that he will never have to exercise the 100 call. After all, people buy insurance and hope they do not have to collect on it—it's there only in case it is needed. If

DEF does go down and Ralph is able to cover at a lower price, his overall profit will be reduced by the $400 he paid for the unused call. That $400 is his insurance cost. On the other hand, while the option is in force, Ralph can lose no more than $700 overall, no matter how high DEF goes in price. If DEF shoots way up to 135, Ralph can exercise his call at 100 and thus buy back the borrowed shares to close out his short position. He sold the stock for $9,700 (100 @ 97) and bought it back for $10,000 (by exercising his 100 call), limiting his loss on the sale and buyback to $300. He also paid $400 for the call, so his overall maximum loss would be $700. Even if DEF went to 150, 200, or even higher, Ralph can lose no more than $700 while his 100 call is in force. His "cost" for this loss limitation is the price of the option.

The purchase of a call can also be used to protect an already-established profit on a short position. James Treanor, a bear on NFW, shorted 100 shares at 82, for $8,200. He was exactly right in his projection about the future course of NFW's price, and it then declined to 58. Jim now has a "paper" profit of $2,400 because he can cover his short for only $5,800. He is reluctant to take his profit now because he thinks NFW will decline still further in price, giving him an even larger profit. Here's his problem: He wants to stay short to increase his profit, but he would hate to see NFW go back up in price and thus erase some or all of the potential profit he already has. To protect most of his profit to date, Mr. Treanor might now buy an NFW 60 call, say for 1.00. If NFW continues to decline, Jim will increase his profit further, but if NFW goes way up, Jim can always exercise his 60 call, thus covering his short position. Once he owns the 60 call, he can always exercise it at that price, whatever the actual market price of NFW might then be, and thus be guaranteed an overall profit of $2,100. He shorted at 82 and now has the right to cover (to buy) at 60, which will give him a trading profit of $2,200. That will be reduced by the cost of the option ($100) so that Jim's net minimum profit will be $2,100. Jim could have taken a $2,400 profit by simply covering his short at 58, but he decided to stay short at a "cost" of giving up $300 of the potential profit, because it gave him the opportunity to eventually cover the short at a still lower price.

COVERED CALL WRITING
FOR ADDITIONAL INCOME

Thus far we have been referring to uncovered call writing. Selling (writing) such calls is a relatively speculative activity engaged in by those who envision a steady or declining market. Other, more conservative investors might be inclined to write *covered* calls in an attempt to increase the returns from their investments. Here is a typical example: Mrs. Rosemary Monaghan is long (owns) 1,000 shares of IBM. She bought the stock at a much lower level than its present price per share of 102.40, but she thinks its price will remain about the same for the next few weeks. Rosemary might sell 10 IBM 110 calls expiring in two weeks for 1.75 each, taking in $1,750 (10 calls @ $175 each). Since she is long the underlying stock, she is a *covered* writer. If IBM stays below 110 for the life of the calls, Mrs. Monaghan will keep the $1,750 premium she received and will still be long the stock. If IBM pays a dividend during this time, she keeps that too. Rosemary is under an obligation to sell her 1,000 IBM at 110 per share if asked to do so, but that will not happen unless IBM goes above 110. Here are three outcomes for Mrs. Monaghan:

1. If IBM stays under 110 for the life of the options, she will retain the premium of $1,750 and still own her 1,000 IBM. She might then consider selling other IBM calls in an attempt to repeat the process.

2. If IBM goes above 110, she will be exercised and must hand over her 1,000 IBM at 110 per share. But is that the bad news? She bought IBM at a much lower price, then received $1,750 in premiums (in addition to any dividends she may also have received), and then sold her stock through exercise at 110. What Rosemary did "lose" through this covered call writing approach was her ability to profit from any amount by which IBM might sell *above* 110 during the options' life. If it goes above 110 she will be called, and the buyer of the calls will make any further profit. This was an acceptable risk to Rosemary because she believed IBM would not sell above 110 while the options were in force. Isn't she in an odd position? She owns IBM, but probably does not want it to go above 110 while the options are alive. If she is correct, and IBM stays under 110, Rosemary can have her cake (she will still own her IBM stock) and eat it too (she earned an extra $1,750).

3. Mrs. Monaghan can always trade out of the options by buying them back. She sold (shorted) 10 IBM 110 call options and has the ability to cover them in the open market by buying 10 such options with the same expiration month. Her position with respect to options would then be flat and she would have no further obligations. She cannot buy them back after she has received an exercise notice, however, as it would then be too late. Rosemary might have a profit or a loss on her sale and buyback of the options, depending on whether she was able to buy them back above 1.75 (she would have a loss) or below 1.75 (she would have a profit).

THE RISKS AND REWARDS OF CALL BUYING AND CALL WRITING

A *call buyer* can lose no more than the premium he or she pays, and has an unlimited profit potential.

An *uncovered call writer* can make no more than the premium he or she receives, and has an unlimited loss potential.

A *covered call writer* risks having his or her stock called away, thus preventing him or her from profiting by a rise in the stock above the call strike price.

Reasons for Utilizing Call Options

Hedge	**Speculation**
Buying calls to protect against runaway losses on short positions or to protect already-established profits on short positions.	Writing calls when clients' market expectations are flat or bearish; buying calls when clients' market expectations are bullish.

SUMMARY

Call buyers are bullish and uncovered call writers are bearish. What the buyer makes, the seller loses. What the buyer loses, the seller makes. Buyers and sellers have the same breakeven points.

Call options can be utilized in a number of ways. Buyers can use them as a means of participating in a bull movement with a relatively small initial investment (leverage). Investors can buy call options to protect a short position against a catastrophic loss, or to protect an already-established profit on a short position (hedging).

Uncovered call writers can speculate on the direction of the market. They will profit when and if prices are stable or go down, a dangerous game when you consider that they can make only a small profit (the premium they receive when they sell the option) but are exposed to the possibility of a large loss.

Covered calls may be sold by investors who are trying to augment their portfolio income by retaining option premiums while also receiving dividends on their holdings.

MULTIPLE-CHOICE QUIZ

Utilize the following information to answer questions 1 to 3:

Mr. Adam Davids shorts 100 shares of YAC at 83.00 and at the same time buys a YAC 85 call for 4.00.

1. What is Mr. Davids' maximum profit potential?
   a. $7,900
   b. $8,100
   c. $8,900
   d. unlimited

2. What is Adam's maximum loss exposure?
   a. $600
   b. $7,900
   c. $8,100
   d. unlimited

3. What is Mr. Davids' breakeven point? (When the option expires, what market price for YAC will permit Adam to break even?)
   a. 79.00
   b. 81.00
   c. 87.00
   d. 89.00

Answer questions 4 and 5 using the following information:

Mrs. Lynda Petruski writes an uncovered NFW 85 call at 4.50.

4. What is Lynda's maximum profit potential?
   a. $450
   b. $8,050
   c. $8,950
   d. unlimited

5. What is Mrs. Petruski's maximum loss potential?
   a. $450
   b. $8,050
   c. $8,950
   d. unlimited

PRACTICE EXERCISES

What are the maximum profit potential, the maximum loss exposure, and the breakeven point for each of the following option positions? All short calls are uncovered (naked). Show profit and loss potential in dollars (not points) and show the breakeven in points (not dollars).

1.   long 1 ABC April 45 call @ 3.50

2.   short 1 DEF May 60 call @ 2.00

3.   long 10 GHI October 25 calls @ 1.25

4.   short 10 JKL January 105 calls @ 5.00

5.   long 5 MNO July 80 calls @ 6.65

6.   short 5 PQR February 35 calls @ .50

MULTIPLE-CHOICE ANSWERS AND EXPLANATIONS

1. **a.** Mr. Davids is a bear—that's why he shorted the stock—and he wants the stock to go way down in price. If it goes down as far as possible, it will go to zero. Mr. Davids can then buy back for nothing the stock he sold at 83, thus making $8,300 on the sell/buy trades. This profit will be offset in part by the cost of the unused call option he bought for insurance ($400), reducing his potential overall profit to $7,900.

2. **a.** All he can lose is $600. Having shorted (sold) the stock at 83, the worst he can do is to buy it back at 85 (that's why he bought the 85 call). He will lose $200 on the sell/buy trades, plus the cost of the option ($400), for a total maximum loss potential of $600.

3. **a.** Adam paid $400 for the option. He will break even if, at expiration, the stock is down 4 points from where he sold it. Then he can cover the short for a 4-point profit that exactly offsets the 4-point cost of the option.

4. **a.** An option writer's maximum profit potential is the price she receives for the option. That's as good as it's going to get for Lynda, who is hoping that NFW does not go above the 85 strike price during the call's life. She then gets to retain the entire premium of $450.

5. **d.** There is no limit to how much Lynda might lose. On a practical level, she would probably trade out of the option if the stock started to skyrocket, keeping her loss within manageable limits.

ANSWERS TO PRACTICE EXERCISES

	Maximum Profit	Maximum Loss	Breakeven
1.	unlimited	$350	48.50
2.	$200	unlimited	62.00
3.	unlimited	$1,250	26.25
4.	$5,000	unlimited	110.00
5.	unlimited	$3,325	86.65
6.	$250	unlimited	35.50

Long calls (questions 1, 3, 5) have an unlimited profit potential because, at least in theory, there is no limit to how high a stock can trade. Short naked calls (questions 2, 4, 6) have an unlimited loss exposure for the same reason.

The most one can lose on a long call is the amount paid (the premium). The most one can gain on a short call is the amount received (the premium).

The breakeven point for a call is the same for both the buyer and the writer—the strike (exercise) price plus the premium. At that point the buyer receives back what she paid for the option, and the seller gives back what she received for the option.

CHAPTER 14

Put Options, Straddles, and Spreads

PUT OPTIONS

Put options give their owners the right to *sell* stock at a set price. While put option holders have this right, they do not have any obligations—they may exercise their options, but they are not forced to do so. Listed put options are traded on the same exchanges as are call options: the Chicago Board Options Exchange (CBOE), the American Stock Exchange, the Philadelphia Stock Exchange, the International Securities Exchange, and the Pacific Stock Exchange.

A typical put option might read: 1 IBM Oct 110 put. This option grants its owner the right to sell 100 shares of IBM common stock at 110 per share until late next October. Let's examine each part of the description.

1 *IBM Oct 110 put*—The "1" indicates that this is one put that conveys the right to sell 100 shares of stock. Every put option carries the right to sell 100 shares of stock. Three puts would permit the sale of 300 shares, and 15 puts would cover 1,500 shares.

1 **IBM** *Oct 110 put*—IBM is the underlying stock, the stock that the put holder has the right to sell.

1 IBM **Oct** *110 put*—This option expires late in October. There will be other outstanding IBM 110 puts expiring in other months.

1 IBM Oct **110** *put*—The strike price, or exercise price, is 110. There may be other Oct IBM puts outstanding with higher and lower strike prices (100, 105, 115, 120).

1 IBM Oct 110 **put**—This is the type of option, which gives its owner the right to sell stock. (A call permits its owner to buy stock.)

Time Value and Intrinsic Value

If the current price of IBM in the open market is 108, and an IBM 110 put is trading at a premium of 12.50 (that's $1,250 for one put option), it is in-the-money by 2 points and has a time value of 10.50 points. Here's the logic: The option has 2 points of intrinsic value because its owner can sell stock at 110 at a time when that stock's open market price is 108. Being able to sell 2 points higher than market results in an in-the-money value (intrinsic value) of 2. Since the option's price (its premium) is 12.50, it is selling for 10.50 points more than its intrinsic value (12.50 − 2), and that 10.50 points represents time value.

Why Buy Puts?

Long puts represent a bearish position. Since the owner of the put has the right to sell stock at a fixed price, he or she wants the underlying stock to decline in value. If the stock sells well below the put's strike price, the put owner can buy stock at that low price and exercise the put at the higher strike price. A long put may be considered an alternative to a short sale for an investor who believes a stock will decline in price.

PUT OPTIONS AS A BEARISH STRATEGY

There is a dramatic difference in the amount of potential profit and the amount of potential loss to be enjoyed or suffered by buying a put rather than selling short. Let's compare how a bearish investor might attempt to profit from a downturn in the price of what he believes to be an overvalued stock, either by selling short or by buying puts.

The first approach might be to sell short 100 shares of XYZ at 98. If XYZ goes bankrupt (which is what our bearish investor is hoping for, at best), the investor will make $9,800. Having sold the stock short at 98 (100 @ 98 = $9,800), he can cover the short by buying back for zero (the stock is bankrupt) and thus make the entire difference. But what if XYZ doesn't go down in price, but rather goes up, way up? Our short seller will someday have to cover the short to close out the position. He delivered borrowed stock against the short sale and is under an obligation to buy that stock in order to return the borrowed shares. There is (at least in theory) no limit to how high the stock can go, and therefore no limit to how much our short seller might lose. A short seller is limited in the amount of profit he might make because the stock can go down only to zero, but he has an unlimited loss exposure because there is no limit to how high a stock can go.

An alternative approach to profit from a market decline in a given security is to buy a put on that stock. We will use the same stock as in the short sale example—XYZ, which is trading at 98. Rather than shorting the stock, we will buy a 95 XYZ put for, let us say, 4.50. The put is out-of-the-money and has no intrinsic value. (Do you agree? Work it out: To exercise a put by selling stock at 95 when it's trading in the open market for 98 doesn't make any sense.) The entire premium, 4.50, is time value. If XYZ goes bankrupt—if the stock declines to zero—the put owner will make an overall profit of $9,050 on his modest investment. (He can buy the stock for zero and exercise the put at 95. He paid $450 for the put and can exercise for $9,500.) Note that the maximum potential profit for the put buyer is a little less than the short seller's maximum profit potential. The most dramatic difference in the two approaches is in the investor's exposure to loss. The put buyer can lose only the premium he paid for the put, in this case $450, while the short seller has an unlimited loss exposure.

PUT OPTIONS AS A HEDGE

Puts may also be purchased to protect against a large loss on a long position, or to protect an already-established profit on a long position.

For example, Mrs. Joan Bradley buys 100 shares of RQF at 82. She is bullish on RQF and expects it to rise in price. She has an unlimited profit potential, but she has a loss exposure of $8,200 (if RQF were to go bankrupt). Joan might also buy, as a type of insurance, an RQF 80 put for, let's say, 3.00. This put is her protection against a dramatic decline in the price of RQF. She hopes she does not have occasion to exercise the put, as she wants the stock to go up in price. If RQF declines dramatically in price, Joan can exercise her put and sell the stock for 80. This limits her loss to $500—the $200 difference between her purchase price (82) and her sale price (she puts the stock at 80), plus the $300 cost of the put. This is her protection during the life of the put. If she still owns the stock after the put expires, she is then at risk for the full amount of the investment. Remember, she is bullish and is rooting for a high price on the stock. She owns the put as a hedge against a large decline in the market price of RQF.

If Mrs. Bradley had a large profit on another long position—say she had bought 1,000 shares of POS at 55 and it had risen to 83—she might now buy 10 puts, with an 80 strike, to protect most of her already-established profit. With the stock at 83, Joan has a "paper" profit of 28 points, or $28,000. She is still bullish on the stock and expects it to go even higher, but she wants protection against the stock declining in value and thus eroding some or all of her profit to date. Joan's insurance policy is her 10-put position. Even if POS goes down substantially, Joan can exercise her puts (while they are still in force) and effectively sell at 80. Presuming that the puts were purchased at 2.00, Joan is assured of a profit of at least $23,000, no matter how low POS declines. At any time before her options expire, she can put the stock at 80, irrespective of its then-current market price. Having bought for 55 and being assured of a sale price of 80, she will have a $25,000 trading profit, reduced by the cost of the 10 puts (10 × $200), or a net profit of $23,000. Again, Joan does *not* want to have to exercise the puts. She would rather that the stock kept going up in price so she could eventually sell her 1,000 shares well above 83. She purchased the puts only for insurance.

STRADDLES

A straddle consists of a call *and* a put on the same stock, with the same strike prices and expiration months. Buying a BCD July 40 call and a BCD July 40 put would constitute a long straddle. Selling an EFG August 65 call and an EFG August 65 put would make up a short straddle.

The owner of a straddle benefits from any movement of the underlying stock from the strike price, up or down. If the stock goes down, the *put* goes in-the-money; if the stock goes up, the *call* goes in-the-money.

Presuming the underlying stock goes way down, the put side of the straddle will benefit. If the stock goes to zero, the BCD 40 put will be worth 40 because the holder can buy the stock in the open market for zero and put it (exercise the put) at 40. If the entire premium for the straddle (both the put and the call) had been 6.00 ($600), then the investor's profit would be $3,400. If, instead, the stock goes above the strike price, the call will become valuable. As with any long call, there is (at least in theory) an unlimited profit potential. The holder's maximum profit potential is unlimited, the maximum loss exposure is $600 (the premium paid), and the breakeven points are 34 and 46. Yes, that's correct, there are *two* breakeven points. If the stock goes up to 46, the call will be worth $600, exactly offsetting the straddle's purchase price. If the stock goes down to 34, the put will be worth $600, again offsetting the straddle's purchase price. The investor benefits, point for point, if the stock goes above 46 or below 34.

The buyer of a straddle believes that the price of the stock will fluctuate, either up or down, and she wants to be able to benefit from a move in *either* direction. The seller (writer) of a straddle hopes that the stock does *not* fluctuate in price. The maximum profit potential for the straddle writer is the premium received; his maximum loss exposure is unlimited if the short call is naked.

SPREADS

A sophisticated options strategy involves spreads. There are many types of spreads, but we will describe only two—bull spreads and bear spreads.

This is a *bull spread*: **long 1 FDS May 55 call and short 1 FDS May 65 call.** Unlike a straddle, this spread consists of a *long* call and a *short* call, with *different* strike prices. Presuming that the spreader paid 5 for the long call and received 3 for the short call, he has a net debit of $200—the $500 he paid for the 55 call, offset in part by the $300 he received for selling the short call. If, while the options are alive, FDS goes to 65, the long 55 call will be worth at least 10 as it will be 10 points in-the-money. At that point the investor's profit will be $800: the $1,000 the call will be worth minus the $200 net cost of the spread. Notice that if FDS goes *higher* than 65, the investor will not benefit further. For every point above 65, additional gains on the long call will be offset by similar losses on the short call. Above 65, both calls are in-the-money and whatever the spreader then gains on his long call he will lose on his short call. His maximum profit potential is $800, his maximum loss exposure is $200, and his breakeven point is 57. If FDS stays below 55, both options expire worthless and the investor's loss is the initial net debit. If, at expiration, FDS is at 57, the long call will be worth 2, the short call will be worthless, and the spreader will have recouped his initial net investment. In a bull spread, as in this example, the strike price of the long option is *lower* than the strike price of the short option.

This is a *bear spread*: **long 1 WEF June 95 call and short 1 WEF June 90 call.** Note that the strike price of the long option is *higher* than the strike price of the short option. As a 95 call will sell at a cheaper price than a 90 call, the spreader will have a net credit after laying on the spread. With this spread, the investor is hoping the price of the underlying stock will go down below the strike price of the short option. Both options will then expire worthless, and the investor will thus retain the going-in credit.

There are spreads involving different strike prices (price or vertical spreads), as in our two examples, and spreads involving different expiration months (time or horizontal spreads). An almost limitless variety of spreads is available, with exotic names including condors and butterflies, but they are beyond the scope of this introductory text. Generally, spreads have rather limited profit potentials and loss exposures.

Reasons for Utilizing Put Options

Hedge	Speculation
Buying puts to protect against runaway losses on long positions and to protect already-established profits on long positions.	Writing puts when investors are bullish on the market and buying puts when investors are bearish on the market.

SUMMARY

Short uncovered calls have the greatest loss exposure (unlimited), while short puts are exposed to a large (but finite) loss, the difference between the strike price and zero.

A put gives its owner the *right to sell* stock; the put writer has an *obligation to buy* stock if exercised. Put options have many uses. Puts can be purchased to take advantage of a declining market, without the unlimited loss exposure of short selling, or they can be used to limit the loss on a newly-established long position or to protect an already-established paper profit on a long position.

Straddles consist of a put and a call on the same stock, with the same strike prices and expiration dates. Long straddles benefit from price movement away from the strike price. Spreads generally consist of both long and short positions, with different terms.

MULTIPLE-CHOICE QUIZ

Answer questions 1 to 3 utilizing the following information:

John Gallagher purchases an April GHF 45 put at 2.75.

1. What is John's maximum profit potential?
    a. $275
    b. $4,225
    c. $4,500
    d. $4,775

2. What is John's maximum loss exposure?
    a. $275
    b. $4,225
    c. $4,500
    d. $4,775

3. What is John's breakeven point?
    a. 2.75
    b. 42.25
    c. 45.00
    d. 47.25

Answer questions 4 and 5 utilizing the following information:

An investor has the following straddle: long 1 DFR August 55 call and long 1 DFR August 55 put. The total premium paid for both positions was 5.50.

4. What is her maximum profit potential?
    a. $550
    b. $4,950
    c. $5,550
    d. unlimited

5. What is her maximum loss exposure?
    a. $550
    b. $4,950
    c. $5,550
    d. unlimited

PRACTICE EXERCISES

What are the maximum profit potential, the maximum loss exposure, and the breakeven point for each of the following option positions? Show profit and loss potential in dollars (not points) and show the breakeven in points (not dollars).

1.   long 1 STU June 50 put @ 2.00

2.   short 1 VWX March 85 put @ 3.50

3.   long 5 YZA January 105 puts @ 11.00

4.   short 20 BCD November 25 puts @ .25

5.   short 10 EFG October 90 puts @ 7.40

6.   long 15 HIJ February 65 puts @ 4.90

MULTIPLE-CHOICE ANSWERS AND EXPLANATIONS

1. **b.** A long put is a bearish position—the put holder wants the stock to go down. How far down can a stock go? It could go to zero. In that case (however unlikely), the put holder can buy in the open market for zero and can then put (sell) the stock at 45, making 45 points on the trade ($4,500). Don't forget that the cost of buying the put ($275) reduces the overall maximum profit potential to $4,225.

2. **a.** The most the option buyer can lose is the cost of the option, $275. Keep in mind that the option holder has the right to do something, but is not under any obligation to do anything. The worst-case scenario for the buyer of an option, any option, is that he or she will lose the premium.

3. **b.** The put buyer paid $275 for the option. To recover that investment, the underlying stock has to go down 2.75 points. The option will then be 2.75 points in-the-money and can be sold for that amount, thus recouping the original investment. Alternatively, the option holder might buy stock in the open market at 42.25 and then put the stock so acquired at 45.

4. **d.** Since the position includes a long call, there is (at least in theory) no limit as to the profit that might be made. A stock can go down only to zero, but there is no upside limit.

5. **a.** The worst an option purchaser can do is to have the option expire worthless. She will then lose the premium paid, but never any more than that.

ANSWERS TO PRACTICE EXERCISES

		Maximum Profit	Maximum Loss	Breakeven
1.		$4,800	$200	48.00
2.		$350	$8,150	81.50
3.		$47,000	$5,500	94.00
4.		$500	$49,500	24.75
5.		$7,400	$82,600	82.60
6.		$90,150	$7,350	60.10

Long puts (questions 1, 3, 6) have a per-put profit potential of the strike price minus the premium. Short puts (questions 2, 4, 5) have that same amount as their loss exposure.

The most one can lose on a long put is the amount paid for the put (the premium). The most one can gain on a short put is the amount received for the put (the premium).

The breakeven point for a put is the same for both the buyer and the writer—the strike (exercise) price minus the premium. At that point the buyer receives back what she paid for the option, and the seller gives back what she received for the option.

The Primary Market

In the *primary market*, new issues are sold to the investing public, with the proceeds of the sale flowing through to the issuing corporation. We are concerned here with *new* issues of stocks and bonds. One of Wall Street's most important functions is to facilitate the generation of capital for corporations and governments through this process.

THE SECURITIES ACT OF 1933

The Securities Act of 1933 was enacted to assure that prospective investors receive full and fair disclosure in all *new* security offerings. When a new issue comes to market, the issuer must file a rather large and complex *registration statement* with the Securities and Exchange Commission (SEC). The facts constituting *full and fair disclosure* should be contained in this document, and the SEC examines it carefully to see that it contains enough information so that an informed investor can arrive at a decision as to whether to purchase the new issue. It is quite important to appreciate that *the SEC does not approve nor disapprove a new issue*. It merely examines the registration statement for apparent completeness. Its job is to try to ensure that the public is being given sufficient information. The SEC will take at least 20 days to examine the registration statement; this is known as the *cooling period*. If it determines that the information as submitted is sufficient, the issue can be brought to market after the 20 days. If the SEC takes exception to the information presented, it may ask for clarification or additional information on one or several points. In that case, the cooling period is extended until the issuer satisfies any issues raised by the SEC.

THE PRELIMINARY PROSPECTUS

A document is produced during the waiting period that is essentially a shortened version of the registration statement filed with the SEC. This is the *preliminary prospectus*, popularly known as a "red herring" by virtue of the red lettering down the left side of the cover page which indicates that the information is subject to change and that the issue might not ever come to market. The red herring does not show the price of the new issue—that will be determined just prior to the issue's release—but it sometimes shows a range of prices within which the new issue might be offered. During the cooling period, the only document that may be distributed to prospective purchasers is the red herring. No orders may be taken, and no prospective purchaser can be guaranteed a specific number of shares or bonds. Indications of interest may be noted, but they are just that—indications of interest.

THE FINAL PROSPECTUS

Immediately after the new issue is released, a *final prospectus* is printed, replacing the red herring. This document shows the offering price and will be presented to every buyer of the new issue.

A most important legend on the prospectus states, in part :

THESE SECURITIES HAVE NOT BEEN APPROVED NOR DISAP-PROVED BY THE SECURITIES AND EXCHANGE COMMISSION, NOR HAS THE COMMISSION PASSED UPON THE ACCURACY OR ADE-QUACY OF THE INFORMATION CONTAINED HEREIN. ANY REPRE-SENTATION TO THE CONTRARY IS A CRIMINAL OFFENSE.

The statement sounds serious, and it *is* serious. The SEC does not put a stamp of approval or a "grade A" sticker on any new issue. It simply says: "We took a look at the registration statement and we believe the issuer has supplied sufficient information. Buyer beware; you're on your own."

THE UNDERWRITING PROCESS

While it is possible that the issuer of the securities (the corporation) might attempt to sell its new shares or bonds directly to investors, the usual course of action is to sell the entire issue, at wholesale prices, to a group of brokerage firms (an underwriting syndicate). These brokerage firms buy the new security, usually paying the issuer in full at the wholesale price, and then attempt to sell the issue to the investing public at a slightly higher "retail" price. If they are successful, they earn the spread between the two prices, which is their gross profit on such deals. That is the essence of *underwriting*: buying a new security directly from the issuer at a given price and then attempting to resell to investors, both individuals and institutions, at a higher price.

The specialized type of underwriting used to guarantee the success of a rights offering is known as a standby underwriting and was described at length in Chapter 3.

GOING PUBLIC—INITIAL PUBLIC OFFERINGS (IPOs)

Small companies generally *go public* once they have grown in size. Virtually every large company is publicly held, meaning that its common shares (ownership securities) are available in the open market. The major exceptions to this are the few remaining large accounting firms (once known as the Big Eight before they began merging, one with the other), specialist firms on the major stock exchanges, and a few large investment banking firms. Except for such organizations, almost any large company you can name is publicly held and has gone through the underwriting process. An *initial public offering* (IPO) is just that, a first-time offering of a company's shares to the investing public. In recent years, Wall Street's underwriting firms have raised between $40 billion and $50 billion annually for first-time issues.

BEST EFFORTS—ALL-OR-NONE

With few exceptions, small, little-known companies generally shop around for an underwriter to bring their securities to market. This is known as a *negotiated deal*, as the issuer is free to deal with the underwriter of its choice, the one with whom it negotiates an arrangement. Some smaller underwriting firms specialize in this type of offering since, generally speaking, the larger investment banking firms deal only with better-established and better-known companies. A common type of underwriting arrangement for first-time-around offerings is the *best efforts deal*. Under such an arrangement, the underwriter does *not* purchase all the shares from the issuer, but rather buys only as many new shares from the issuer as it is able to resell, effectively only "taking down" shares if and when it finds buyers. One might argue that this is not a true underwriting because the brokerage firm is not acting as a principal (positioning securities, at risk), but rather is acting as a dealer. Under such an arrangement, only a portion of the entire issue might be sold; the underwriters use their "best efforts" to sell as many of the shares as they are able.

A common variation to the best efforts arrangement is the *best efforts–all-or-none deal*. Under this system, any shares that are sold will be returned to the issuer, with the buyers getting their money back, if the entire issue is not sold. The issuer's stance is, "If you can't sell *all* the shares, don't sell any." One reason the issuer might go this route is because it would be unable to expand its operations with only a portion of the proceeds of the planned issue. After all, building only half of a new factory might not be practical.

AN IPO (THE PRIMARY MARKET)

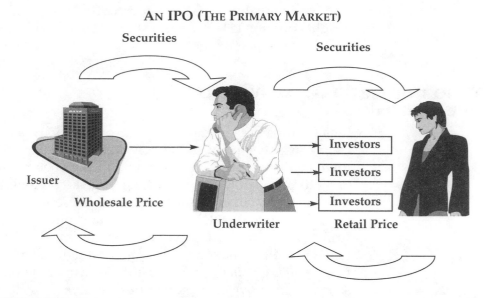

PRIVATE PLACEMENTS

In many instances, an underwriter may be able to place an entire new issue with just one (or several) large investors, usually institutions. Such underwritings are not offered to the general public, but are sold privately to a small, select group of sophisticated purchasers. Such offerings do not have to be registered with the SEC as do public offerings. The securities are usually purchased by institutions for investment, and not for resale. The offering is often tailored to the requirements of the buying institutions, effectively creating a custom-made issue.

COMPETITIVE UNDERWRITINGS

Many large offerings of new issues are done on a *competitive* basis. The issuer announces to the underwriting fraternity its intention to float a new issue, thus soliciting bids from competing underwriting groups. The group offering the issuer the best terms will win the deal. To compete for the issue, several major *investment banking* firms (companies that specialize in bringing new issues to market through the underwriting process) will form in a group with brokerage firms to help them bid for the issue and, if the group is the successful bidder, to help them resell the issue. These groups, each headed by a different major underwriter (the *managing underwriter*), are known as *bidding syndicates*. Syndicates can be quite large, sometimes involving scores of different firms.

Each of the competing underwriting groups holds several private meetings prior to the date the bid is due. They discuss pricing ideas within the group so as to be best prepared to submit a bid that is high enough to win—but low enough so that the investing public will buy the security. The prospective underwriters utilize the time prior to the bid to solicit *indications of interest* from investors. Institutions expressing an interest might ask for a *circle* on a given number of the shares or bonds to be issued. When the issue is released, the institutions have the right to reject the issue if they think the terms are not adequate, but the circle gives them virtual assurance that they will be able to buy the issue if they want to.

Underwriting Brackets

Each bidding syndicate, possibly composed of more than 100 different brokerage firms, is subdivided into *brackets*. The firms in each bracket have a similar underwriting commitment for a certain number of shares or bonds. In a large bond offering, the firms in the topmost bracket might each be responsible for placing $3,000,000 of bonds, those in the second bracket might be underwriting $2,000,000 of the issue, and so on down the line. Those in the lowest bracket might only have $100,000 to place. Notice that the firms' names in the *tombstone* (described in the next section) are arranged in several different alphabetized groups, with each separate group listing firms that have progressively smaller underwriting commitments.

The Tombstone

Just after a bidding syndicate wins a new issue, it publishes a specialized announcement in the financial press. This is known as a *tombstone*, so called because it is usually in the shape of an upright rectangle, like a tombstone in a cemetery. It is, effectively, an advertisement. The number of shares in the offering or the par value of the bonds is shown, as well as the per-share or per-bond price. The name of the managing underwriter(s) comes next, followed by the remaining members of the syndicate, in alphabetical order, by bracket. Note, in our sample tombstone on the next page, that William J. Mahan & Co. is the managing underwriter and that three separate underwriting brackets are listed: Gneiding Brothers is a top-bracket underwriter, with Stacy and Co. in the bracket below, and Belding Inc. in the lowest bracket.

The tombstone announcement is neither an offer to sell, nor a solicitation of an offer to buy, any securities.

The Pot and Hot Deals

The managing underwriter holds back some of each underwriter's shares (or bonds), approximately 25%, for sales to institutional buyers. This is known as the *pot*. If all of these shares are purchased, it is a very encouraging sign (as it shows big demand from big buyers) and the managing underwriter will be happy to announce, "The pot is clean!"

When a newly issued security is immediately snapped up, exhausting the supply available at the initial offering price, the offering is known as a *hot deal*. The initial demand not having been satisfied, the new security will sell at an immediate premium in the secondary market. This is similar to ticket sales for a popular concert: People were queued up at the box office

<u>New Issue</u>

March 26, 2003

$ 25,000,000

Rangle Corporation

9 3/4% Subordinated Debentures due 2023

Price 100%

Copies of the Prospectus may be obtained in any State from such of the undersigned as may legally offer these securities in compliance with the securities laws of such State.

William J. Mahan & Co.

Anberg Inc.	Caldwell & Co. Inc.	Gneiding Brothers	Jadell Co.
Lastey & Fader, Inc.	Opperfell, Inc.	Reynaud Corp.	Victrin & Co.
Blauvelt Inc.	Farnsworth & Assoc.	Peridot Bros.	Stacy & Co.

Umbertill and Gallagher Inc.   Wellingford Incorporated

Babcock & Dresdner, Inc.   Bartolo Co.   Belding Inc.   Natterson & Assoc.

Patrician and Georgeson Inc.   Telleride Brothers

well before it opened, and the concert tickets sold out immediately after they went on sale. Those who were unable to buy tickets at the box office paid much higher than face-value prices to scalpers. Underwriters are strictly prohibited from holding back shares when there is unsatisfied demand. They are required by law to sell the shares at no more than the agreed-upon initial offering price.

The managing underwriter is permitted to *stabilize* a new issue by placing bids at or slightly under the public offering price. The intent is to prevent the open-market price from falling far below the public offering price before the new issue is sold. This is a legalized form of *pegging the market*. Of course, this action would not be necessary if the issue were a hot deal; it is usually utilized only for issues that are slow to sell. Please keep in mind that underwriting normally involves brokerage firms acting in a *principal* capacity. They position the new security, and are at risk in that they might not be able to resell some or all of the new issue at the public offering price. When an issue fails to sell at the public offering price, the managing underwriter might "break" the syndicate, telling members: "You're on your own. You can sell the new issue at whatever price you can get. Good luck." Such sales are sometimes effected well below the public offering price, occasionally even lower than the price the underwriters paid the issuer (the wholesale price), but in no event are the brokerage firms permitted to sell the issue at any price *higher* than the public offering price.

The Selling Group

The winning underwriting group will sometimes make shares available at a professional discount to brokerage firms outside the syndicate, even to those firms who were competing with them to win the issue. This is done in the hope that the same professional courtesy will be extended to the winning bidders of this issue when they come up the losers on a subsequent deal. The entire group of brokerage firms involved in selling the issue, the underwriters in the syndicate as well as any outside firms that may be involved, is known as the *selling group*.

SUMMARY

The primary market is involved when the proceeds of the sale of new securities flow through to the issuer of the securities. Underwriting is essentially the purchase of new securities by underwriters, from the issuer, at a wholesale price, with the hope that these securities can then be sold to the general public at a higher retail price. Types of underwritings include: standby offerings, negotiated deals, competitive deals, best efforts–all-or-none, and private placements. In recent years, brokerage firms underwrote an average of more than $2 trillion of new issues annually. This money fueled businesses by providing long-term capital.

The primary market is governed by the Securities Act of 1933, the "full disclosure" act. Most new issues can be promoted only through the use of the preliminary prospectus, also called the red herring. The SEC is involved in offerings to the general public. During the minimum of 20 days that it examines the registration statement, it attempts to determine that the issuer has supplied sufficient information to potential purchasers.

MULTIPLE-CHOICE QUIZ

1. New issues trade in the:
   a. listed market
   b. floor-based market
   c. primary market
   d. secondary market

2. The Securities and Exchange Commission _____ new issues.
   a. sometimes approves
   b. sometimes disapproves
   c. always approves or disapproves
   d. neither approves nor disapproves

3. A number of underwriters all sharing the same commitment as to the amount of shares or bonds they will underwrite is known as a (an):
   a. even syndicate
   b. underwriting bracket
   c. best efforts grouping
   d. all-for-one tombstone

4. In underwriting terms, the "pot" refers to the:
   a. total of all the underwriters' antes
   b. number of shares unsold at the end of the underwriting period
   c. portion of the issue reserved for institutional sales
   d. total number of shares to be underwritten

5. A small, relatively unknown company wishing to go public would most likely be brought to market via a:
   a. best efforts–all-or-none deal
   b. competitive offering
   c. standby offering
   d. private placement

PRACTICE EXERCISES

Refer to the tombstone for Rangle Corporation depicted in Chapter 15 to answer these questions.

1. In addition to the managing underwriter, William J. Mahan & Co., how many underwriting brackets are represented in the announcement?

2. What will be the investors' yield to maturity for bonds purchased at the offering price?

3. When did the Securities and Exchange Commission examine the issue?

4. Does the announcement refer to a primary or a secondary offering?

MULTIPLE-CHOICE ANSWERS AND EXPLANATIONS

1. **c.** New issues trade initially in the primary market. Primary market transactions are typified by principal trades (broker at risk) whereby the issuer receives the proceeds of the offering. Once the new issue is distributed, further trades are done in the secondary market, either OTC or on an exchange. The secondary market is where resales of stocks and bonds trade.

2. **d.** This is a most important point. The SEC neither approves nor disapproves new issues. To infer otherwise is a serious violation. The government cannot guarantee any new issue.

3. **b.** Each of the separate alphabetical listings on the tombstone is a bracket. The brokers' level of participation is progressively smaller as they are positioned lower down on the tombstone.

4. **c.** The managing underwriter withholds about 20 to 25% of each underwriter's portion for bulk sales to institutional buyers. When these are sold (when the pot is clean), there is cause for joy among the members of the syndicate.

5. **a.** That's the route usually taken for IPOs of lesser-known companies. Competitive deals are generally reserved for very large offerings of debt securities of public utilities and municipalities, while standby offerings have to do with rights deals.

ANSWERS TO PRACTICE EXERCISES

1. Three

   The first bracket begins with Anberg and ends with Victrin, the second bracket begins with Blauvelt and ends with Wellingford, and the last bracket begins with Babcock & Dresdner and ends with Telleride Bros.

2. 9.75%

   For bonds purchased at par (100% of face value), the current yield and yield to maturity will be the same as the nominal yield (coupon rate).

3. Never

   The SEC neither approves nor disapproves new issues.

4. A primary offering

   Since the issuer is receiving the proceeds of the sale, this is a primary offering. If bonds purchased on the offering are sold into the open market at a later date, those sales will be in the secondary market.

CHAPTER 16

The Secondary Market

The Securities Act of 1933 deals with new issues, the primary market. The Securities Exchange Act of 1934 covers virtually everything else. The 1934 Act created the SEC, giving it dominion over all *self-regulatory organizations* (*SROs*). The 1934 Act deals with the *secondary market*, all marketplaces and exchanges, and the self-regulatory organizations. The major SROs are the National Association of Securities Dealers (the over-the-counter market), the New York Stock Exchange (the listed market), and the Municipal Securities Rulemaking Board (municipal securities). These SROs—NASD, NYSE, and MSRB—cannot change their rules without SEC preapproval.

In secondary market transactions, a security's ownership is transferred from a seller (other than the issuing corporation) to a buyer. Unlike a primary market transaction in which the issuing corporation receives the proceeds of the sale, secondary transactions do not involve the issuer. Here's an analogy: When you purchase a new car, the auto manufacturer delivers a new automobile and receives the purchase price. A car dealer is involved in the transaction, but the auto manufacturer receives the purchase price less the dealer's commission. This is a primary market transaction. If you own the car for several years and then sell it to a neighbor or to a used-car dealer, the auto manufacturer is not in any way involved. This is a secondary market transaction.

THE SECONDARY MARKETPLACES

Secondary market transactions can occur either on an organized exchange or over-the-counter. Any transactions *not* effected on the floor of an organized exchange (the *listed* marketplaces such as the New York Stock Exchange or the American Stock Exchange) are *over-the-counter* (*OTC*). The stocks of the majority of very large corporations trade on one or more of the organized exchanges. New issues, mutual funds, corporate, municipal, and government bonds, and smaller corporations trade OTC. The Nasdaq market (OTC) trades many issues that more than meet the listing requirements of the exchanges. Some of these are very large organizations, known throughout the world, that have elected not to list on an exchange, preferring that their shares trade OTC. Some corporate bonds are listed for exchange trading, but the vast majority of bond trading takes place OTC.

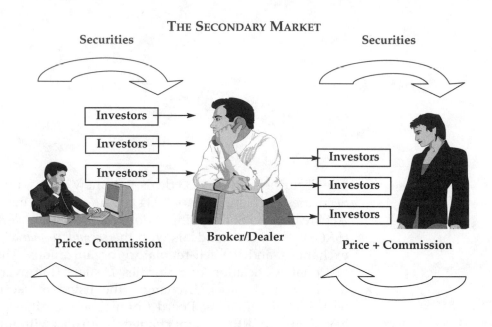

STOCK EXCHANGES—THE LISTED MARKETPLACE

Stock exchanges operate on the *double-auction system*. All interested parties, both buyers and sellers, meet at a single location and trade by open outcry. The New York Stock Exchange uses a *specialist system*. Specialists act as both brokers and dealers, sometimes acting for their own account and risk (principal trades), sometimes handling away-from-the-market orders as an agent for commission-house brokers (agency trades). The specialist firms *make a market* in a number of different issues that have been assigned to them. They must be prepared to buy and sell at all times—that's the essence of making a market. There are a total of 1,366 *seats* on the New York Stock Exchange; this number was set in 1953. Each seat is a membership in the exchange, and only those 1,366 individuals owning seats can actually effect buy or sell orders. Seats are owned by specialists, commission-house brokers, $2 brokers, and registered competitive traders. There are several thousand other people working on the *floor* of the exchange, including support staff for the specialist firms, reporters, and telephone clerks.

PARTICIPANTS IN THE LISTED MARKETPLACE

Each NYSE member firm has at least one partner or vice president who owns a seat on the exchange. Many large firms have as many as 30 or 40 floor partners. These individuals are called *commission-house brokers*. The *$2 brokers*—independent brokers—are not affiliated with a particular brokerage. They execute the overflow of orders from commission-house brokers when the commission-house brokers are too busy to execute the orders themselves. The name stems from the time when they received $2 for each round lot they executed. The fee is no longer $2 per 100 shares (it is now a negotiated, sliding rate), but the name has stuck.

There are three very large rooms that collectively make up the *trading floor* for stocks on the New York Stock Exchange: the Main Room (that's the one you see on TV), the Blue Room, and the Garage. Each of these rooms has one or more *trading posts* where all buys and sells are executed. Each of the several thousand different stock issues that are *listed* (traded) on the NYSE is assigned to a specific trading post. The "Big Board" (as the NYSE is often called) trades the securities of more than 3,500 companies. Most of these are U.S. corporations, but more than 400 are headquartered in about 50 foreign countries. This largest equities market in the world trades securities having a total market capitalization of more than $11 trillion ($11,000,000,000,000).

When an order for a NYSE-listed stock is received by a brokerage firm, it is transmitted to the floor, to one of that firm's "telephone booths." The clerk at the booth summons one of the floor partners who is given the order for execution. The floor partner then goes to the appropriate trading post and executes the order, either with the specialist or with one of the other seat-holders (other commission-house brokers, $2 brokers, or registered competitive traders). After execution, the details of the trade are given to the telephone clerk who reports it back to the brokerage firm. The trade is recorded by a clerk in the executing brokerage's *wire and order room*, who ensures that the report is transmitted to the particular branch office that entered the order. The account executive (registered representative or financial consultant) who entered the order can now call the client with a report. This verbal report will be followed by a written *confirmation* showing the details of the trade. With the tremendous increase in the volume of trading, transactions commonly exceeding two billion shares each day, it is to be expected that most smaller orders are transmitted directly to the trading posts for execution. The NYSE has several automated systems for handling small market orders—the designated order turnaround (DOT) system and the SuperDot system for smaller limit orders.

THE SPECIALIST SYSTEM

All securities are assigned to specialists who are charged with managing the auction process for the stocks in which they specialize. Their duties include:

maintaining a fair and orderly market; providing continuity of prices; narrowing the spread; entering into stabilizing transactions; and acting as a "brokers' broker" for away-from-the-market orders. The specialists act as both brokers and dealers, handling orders for others on a no-risk basis (as brokers) as well as trading for their own accounts (as dealers or market-makers). Specialists are always encouraged to improve the market by bidding and offering for their own accounts. While most trading takes place between various commission-house brokers, $2 brokers, and registered competitive traders, a significant number of trades (including all odd-lot trades) are effected by the specialists. In partial payment for their franchise to specialize in various stocks, the specialists see to it that there is always a fair market—a "two-sided" market—where stocks can be bought and sold at reasonable spreads at any time during trading hours. If no one else is willing to buy, the specialist must buy, and if no one else is willing to sell, the specialist must sell.

THE QUOTATION

A *quote* consists of the highest price anyone is willing to pay for a security—the *bid*—and the lowest price at which anyone is willing to sell—the *offer* (also known as the *asked* price). A typical quote might be: 14.25 bid—14.50 asked. There may be one or more bidders at 14.25, and one or more potential sellers at 14.50. The difference between these two prices is 0.25, the *spread*. Sometimes the bids or offers are made by one or more commission-house brokers, and sometimes the highest bid or lowest offer is being made by the specialist. Specialists cannot compete with other exchange members at a given bid or offer, but they are always encouraged to make the highest bid (or the lowest offer), thus improving the market by narrowing the spread.

Given a quote of 24.65 bid—24.75 offered, at least 100 shares can be sold at no less than 24.65 (the bid), and at least 100 shares can be purchased at no more than 24.75. There are occasions when a trade might be effected at a price within the spread; but for a 100-share trade, you can always sell at no worse than the bid and buy at no worse than the offer.

THE SIZE

Upon request, the specialist will divulge the total number of shares bid for (at the highest bid) and the total number of shares offered (at the lowest offer price). This is known as the *size*. Such information is of interest to a broker attempting to execute an order for more than 100 shares. Without knowledge of the size, she cannot tell how many shares can be bought at the offer price or sold at the bid price. If the quote is 61.35–61.45, with a size of "8 by 11," this means that a total of 8 round lots (800 shares) are bid for at 61.35 and a total of 11 round lots (1,100 shares) are offered at 61.45. The broker now knows that she can sell from 1 to 8 round lots (100 to 800 shares) at the bid price, or can buy from 1 to 11 round lots (100 shares to 1,100 shares) at the offer price.

THE RANGE

A stock's *range* includes most or all of the following information: the price of the opening trade of the day, the high price for the day, the day's low price, the current quotation, the last sale, the trading tick, the day's net change, and the total volume.

Example: The range for XYZ during a given trading day might be the following:

OPEN	**63.40**	The day's first trade was effected at 63.40.
HIGH	**64.05**	The highest-priced trade of the day
LOW	**63.25**	The lowest-priced trade of the day
QUOTATION	**63.35–63.50**	The current quote
LAST	**63.50**	The price of the most recent trade
TICK	**+ tick**	The last *different* price was lower than the last sale of 63.50.
NET CHANGE	**+0.15**	The last sale of 63.50 is 0.15 higher than the previous day's closing price; therefore the previous day's closing price was 63.35.
VOLUME	**128,000 shares**	The total number of shares traded thus far during the trading day

OVER-THE-COUNTER—THE UNLISTED MARKETPLACE

Technically, any trade not executed on the floor of an organized exchange is an over-the-counter (OTC) trade. The OTC (unlisted) market is huge, comprising many thousands of different equity securities and several million debt issues. This is a "negotiated" market, with many competing market-makers rather than a specialist system.

THE NASDAQ STOCK MARKET, INC.

A major national securities market, the Nasdaq Stock Market (developed in 1971), trades the larger, better-known and better-capitalized, non-exchange-traded securities. Like other major national securities markets, Nasdaq has formal listing requirements, electronic trading surveillance, real-time quotations and trade reports, the ability to handle limit orders (described in Chapter 17), and order-routing and execution systems. Nasdaq market-makers are the NASD (National Association of Securities Dealers) member firms that use their own capital to represent a stock and compete with each other to buy and sell the stocks they represent. Nasdaq's structure of competing market-makers differentiates it from the securities exchanges using the specialist (single market-maker) system.

True over-the-counter securities are issues that are not listed either on Nasdaq or on an exchange. These OTC issues are usually smaller and less known than Nasdaq or exchange-traded issues. Many of their quotations are carried in the *pink sheets* published by the National Quotation Bureau, while Nasdaq quotes and detailed trade information are available on a real-time basis through a sophisticated electronic system.

	Specialist	**OTC**
Market-Maker	Single Market-Maker	Multiple Market-Makers
Market Type	Double-Auction Market	Negotiated Market

SUMMARY

After they are initially issued, securities then trade in the public open market. This secondary market consists of about 5,000 listed (exchange-traded) issues and an equal number of issues traded on Nasdaq, with the remaining unlisted issues trading OTC. The OTC market includes many thousands of lesser-known stocks, mutual funds, and virtually all trading in debt issues, including more than one million different municipal issues.

The exchanges operate as a double auction, using the specialist system. The unlisted (Nasdaq and OTC) markets operate on a negotiated basis, using competing market-makers. A quotation is composed of the highest bid and the lowest asking prices, with the difference between the two being known as the spread. Detailed trade information on listed and Nasdaq-traded stocks is carried in the financial press; the prices of smaller issues, primarily foreign stocks, are printed in the pink sheets.

MULTIPLE-CHOICE QUIZ

1. Stock exchanges operate on a _____ system.
    a. negotiated
    b. multiple market-maker
    c. double-auction
    d. range and size

2. Which of the following can effect trades on the New York Stock Exchange?
    I $2 brokers
    II specialists
    III commission-house brokers
    IV registered competitive traders
    a. I and II only
    b. II and III only
    c. I, III, and IV only
    d. I, II, III, and IV

3. Given a quotation of 46.25–46.75 (both bid and offer being made by commission-house brokers), the specialist may:
    a. bid 46.25 and offer at 46.75
    b. bid 46.20 and offer at 46.80
    c. bid 46.30 and offer at 46.70
    d. not bid or offer until after the next trade

4. The "size" indicates:
    a. the highest bid
    b. the lowest offering price
    c. how many shares have traded previously
    d. how many shares are available at the bid and offer

5. Nasdaq trading differs from exchange trading in that Nasdaq:
    a. Operates on a single-auction basis.
    b. Utilizes competing market-makers.
    c. Trades only foreign equities, mutual funds, and debt issues.
    d. Cannot handle limit orders or short sales.

PRACTICE EXERCISES

1. Which of the following own seats on the New York Stock Exchange?
    Commission house brokers
    Registered representatives
    $2 brokers
    Specialists
    Technical analysts
    Fundamental analysts
    Underwriters

2. Do exchange specialists act as brokers or dealers?

Use the following information to answer questions 3 to 5. During the trading day, a stock's range includes the following:

Quotation	34.25 – 34.50
Last Sale	34.40
Net Change	–.25
Size	7 by 9

3. What is the spread on the stock?

4. How many shares can be purchased at the offer price?

5. What was the previous day's closing price?

MULTIPLE-CHOICE ANSWERS AND EXPLANATIONS

1. **c.** The double-auction system is used on the exchanges, with all interested buyers and sellers meeting at the appropriate trading post to execute orders. Traders are all assembled in one place, and communicate by open outcry.

2. **d.** All the parties listed can effect trades. Only those owning one the 1,366 seats are allowed to actually buy and sell. A NYSE seat sold for $2.65 million in 1999.

3. **c.** The specialist can only improve the quote by bidding higher than the crowd (the commission-house brokers and $2 brokers) or by offering at a lower price. He or she cannot make the same bid or offer that already exists (choice a) as that doesn't narrow the spread. He or she cannot enter a lower bid or a higher offer than already exists (choice b) as only the highest bid and lowest offer make up a quote. The specialist is always encouraged to narrow the spread, making for a very liquid market.

4. **d.** The size indicates the number of shares bid for and the number of shares offered. Brokers can "hit" the bid or offer for any or all of the amount of shares indicated in the size. Specialists will usually divulge only the size of the highest bid and lowest offer, not the size of their "book" of away-from-the-market orders.

5. **b.** The essential difference between the exchanges and Nasdaq is that all exchange trading takes place at a single location using the specialist system, while Nasdaq trading is decentralized and uses competing multiple market-makers. Nasdaq is a negotiated market.

ANSWERS TO PRACTICE EXERCISES

1. Commission-house brokers, $2 brokers, and specialists (as well as registered competitive traders) all have NYSE seats. The others listed are all "upstairs" personnel.

2. Specialists act as both brokers and dealers.

   Specialist act as brokers' brokers, handling away-from-the-market orders, and also trade for their own accounts.

3. The spread is $0.25.

   The spread is simply the difference between the bid and the asked prices. One of the specialists' many duties is to keep the spread as narrow as practicable, thus affording fairer and more liquid markets.

4. 900 shares

   The size of 7×9 indicates 700 shares bid for and 900 shares offered.

5. 34.65

   If the latest trade was 34.40, and it was 0.25 less than the previous closing price, the previous closing price must have been 34.65.

CHAPTER 17

Types of Orders

Adding a security to a portfolio through a purchase, or reducing or eliminating a position through a sale, involves an *order*. Entering the proper type of order is quite important, and developing an understanding of the different types of orders is a must for both clients and account executives. There are four basic types of orders: *market, limit, stop,* and *stop limit*.

MARKET ORDERS

A *market order* is executed at the best price available at the time it reaches the appropriate trading area (an exchange floor in the case of listed securities and an over-the-counter trading room for unlisted securities). With very few exceptions, a market order will be executed at or very close to the price of the preceding trade. Given a quotation of 53.05–53.10, a market order to buy 100 shares will be executed at 53.10 (the offer price), while a market order to sell will be executed at 53.05 (the bid price).

A buy market order is written "buy 100 XYZ @ the market" and a sell market order is written "sell 200 ABC @ the market."

A market order is best utilized by investors who are satisfied with a security's current price level. Those who think a stock is fairly priced, whether they are buying or selling, traditionally use market orders rather than risking a non-execution by entering an order "away from" the market. A market order is entered *at* the market.

The vast majority of market orders are executed very quickly, usually within a few minutes. The investor will receive a confirmation of the trade price in short order so that he or she can move quickly to reinvest the sales proceeds or make provision for payment for securities purchased. Market orders are quick and uncomplicated and, if entered with sufficient time remaining in the trading day, are guaranteed to be executed in a timely manner at the best prevailing price.

LIMIT ORDERS

When investors specify the maximum price they are willing to pay for a purchase or the lowest price they are willing to accept for a sale, they are utilizing *limit orders*.

Buy Limit Order   With a quotation of 27.25–27.30, a client wishing to buy at the market would expect an execution at the offer price, 27.30. If the client was not willing to pay the market price, he or she might enter a buy limit at a somewhat lower price, say 26.75. If the security subsequently declines to 26.75, the customer *may* buy at that price (there may be other clients in the order queue whose orders would be executed first). If the security trades at or below 26.74, then the buy limit order definitely *will* be executed and the client will have saved $0.55 per share by purchasing at 26.75 rather than at 27.30. Notice the two "if's." If the stock does not decline to at least 26.75, the client will not purchase the stock at all.

A buy limit order is entered below the market because the client is attempting to purchase the security at less than the current market price. He will do so if the security declines to an appropriate level. The buy limit order referred to in the preceding paragraph would be written "buy 100 YCA @ 26.75."

Sell Limit Order   A sell limit order is entered *above* the market, as the client is attempting to sell at a price higher than the current market. He or she will do so only if the security rises to an appropriate level. Given a quotation of 35.25–35.30, a client would expect a market order to sell to be executed at 35.25. If the client wanted to receive a higher price, say 36.00, then she would enter a sell limit order (written "sell 100 NFW @ 36.00"). If NFW rises to 36.00, the limit order *may* be executed (there might be other orders at that price ahead in the order queue); if it rises to 36.01 or higher, the order *will* be executed. If the stock does not go up to at least 36.00, the order will not be executed.

The inherent weakness of all limit orders is that the investor has no assurance that the buy or sell order will be executed at all. Since the client has established the highest price he or she will pay for a purchase (buy limit) or the lowest price he or she will accept for a sale (sell limit), there will be no execution if the security does not trade down to the limit price for a buy limit or up to the limit price for a sell limit. Investors may be able to buy a stock more cheaply or sell for a higher price by entering a limit rather than a market order, but they are taking the risk that the limit order will not be executed and they might ultimately have to buy at a price higher than the current market or sell at a price lower than the current market.

STOP ORDERS

For listed securities, a *stop order* is a memorandum to the specialist that becomes a market order if and when the stop price is reached or breached. This much misunderstood and underutilized type of order can be a remarkably effective trading tool. Professional securities salespeople should be familiar with this trading tactic, and must be prepared to explain its effective usage to clients.

Buy stop orders are entered above the market. A practical application of the buy stop order would be to hedge a short position against a large loss. For example, an investor is bearish on ABC and sells 200 shares short at 92.00. She hopes that she will be able to cover her short by buying at a lower price, but she is well aware that she is exposed to a large potential loss should ABC go up instead of down as she anticipates. The investor can limit her loss exposure to approximately 3 points by entering a buy stop order at 95.00 (written "buy 200 ABC @ 95.00 stop"). Through this mechanism, the short position will be automatically covered if ABC subsequently trades at or above 95.00. The investor's market order to buy will be entered immediately after the first trade at 95.00 or higher. This will limit the short seller's loss to approximately $600. Having sold short at 92.00, the 200-share short position will be automatically covered (bought in) at about 95.00. If ABC does not rise to 95.00 or higher, no order will be entered and the client will remain short.

Here's another example: XYZ is currently trading at 84.50. An investor utilizes technical analysis as part of his decision-making investment strategy. He believes that if XYZ subsequently trades at 86.00, it will then go substantially higher. He does not want to buy *unless* XYZ trades at or above 86.00. He would enter a buy stop order at 86.00. Only if XYZ trades at 86.00 or higher will his market order be entered. His purchase will be automatic in that the market order to buy will be entered immediately after the first trade of XYZ at or above 86.00. If XYZ does not trade at 86.00 or higher, no order will be entered.

Sell stop orders are entered below the market. A typical use of the sell stop would be to protect a profit on a long position. As an example, Mr. James Treanor purchased 300 shares of YCA some time ago at 47.00, and it is now trading at 69.00. He has a paper profit of $6,600 and is tempted to sell, but he believes that YCA might trade even higher. A market order to sell gets him out of the position now and establishes the profit, but does not afford an opportunity for further profit if YCA trades even higher. He could try to sell at a higher price by entering a limit order, say at a price of 70.00, but then he risks having YCA fall in price and losing his already-established profit. The sell limit order will get Mr. Treanor another point if the stock rises to 70.00 or so, but he risks not selling at all if YCA falls in price. How can Jim both protect most of his profit to date and still remain in a position to benefit from a further rise in the price of YCA? He might enter an order to "sell 300 YCA @ 68.00 stop." His market order to sell 300 YCA will be entered only if YCA declines to 68.00 or lower. If YCA stays above 68.00, Jim will continue to hold the stock and might benefit from a rise in price above 69.00. He can then sell at the higher price (using a market or limit order), remembering of course to cancel the sell stop order. Once the sell stop is entered, Jim has protected most of his profit to date because his position will automatically be sold at about 68.00, if YCA trades at 68.00 or lower. That's Jim's "price" for continuing to hold the long position—at worst he gives up only about a point of his profit to date if the stop order is elected, but he has a chance to add to his profit if the stop order is not elected and YCA trades higher. Jim has hedged most of his profit. He does not have to watch the stock price for any signs of weakness, calling constantly for quotations (that's time-consuming and nerve-wracking). He merely enters the stop order and is assured his position will be liquidated automatically if YCA declines to or through the stop price.

STOP LIMIT ORDERS

A *stop limit order* is a memorandum to the specialist that becomes a limit order if and when the stop price is reached or breached. Stop limit orders can be used for the same purposes as stop orders—to protect profits, to guard against large losses, or to establish positions if certain technical indicators arise—but they have the same basic weakness as do all limit orders: The investor has no assurance that a trade will be effected. An investor might want the same automatic order entry afforded by a stop order, but wants a limit order entered when the stop price is reached or breached, not a market order.

Let's discuss the differences between stop orders and stop limit orders. Both buy stops and buy stop limits are entered above the market. Given a current price level of 70.00 for RFQ, an instruction to "buy 100 RFQ @ 72.00 stop" would become a *market* order immediately after the first trade of RFQ at 72.00 or higher (the electing trade). The order would most probably be executed on the next tick after the electing trade. Admittedly, the following sequence of trades is unrealistic, but we are simply illustrating. Suppose RFQ trades in the following sequence: 70.00, 71.00, 71.50, 72.00 (this trade elects the stop order and the market order would now be entered), 72.25, and subsequent prices still higher. The client would buy 100 shares of RFQ at 72.25. If the client had entered a stop limit order such as "buy 100 RFQ @ 72.00 stop 72.00 limit," the *limit* order would have been entered at the same time (just after the trade at 72.00). But since the stock did not trade again at 72.00, the client would not have gotten an execution.

On some exchanges the limit price on a stop limit instruction need not be the same as the stop price, for example, "sell 500 XYZ @ 35.50 stop, 35.25 limit" or "buy 800 ABC @ 68.75 stop, 69.05 limit."

Entered *Below* the Market	Entered *At* the Market	Entered *Above the* Market
Buy Limit	Buy @ Market	Sell Limit
Sell Stop	Sell @Market	Buy Stop
Sell Stop Limit		Buy Stop Limit

Types of Orders and Their Functions

Market	Limit	Stop	Stop Limit
Order is executed at the best price available in the market at the time that it reaches the trading area.	Specifies the maximum price an investor will pay for a security or the lowest price an investor will sell for.	When the stop price is reached or breached, a *market* order is entered for the sale or purchase of the security.	When the stop price is reached or breached, a *limit* order is entered for the sale or purchase of the security.

ORDER QUALIFIERS AND THEIR EFFECTS

There are certain modifiers that may be added to trading orders. Such specialized instructions are normally used by institutions trading blocks of shares (more than 10,000 shares), and are only rarely utilized by the average individual investor. These special instructions include (among others): all or none, fill or kill, immediate or cancel, not held, and market on close.

All or None (AON)

The all-or-none instruction dictates that an entire purchase or sale must be done at one time. Normally, when you enter an order to buy 10,000 XYZ at a limit, you might receive a report that only part of your order had been executed. In the absence of an all-or-none instruction, you must accept whatever part or parts of the 10,000-share order were executed. If an order is entered AON (all or none), the customer will accept only an execution for the entire block of 10,000 shares, not partial executions. The order says, "I want to buy (or sell) all the stock or none of it. I will not accept anything less than a full execution."

AON orders are in force for the remainder of the trading day on which they are entered. The client will receive one of two messages—either a report that 10,000 shares of XYZ were purchased at or below the limit price or "nothing done"—at the end of the trading day.

The danger is that AON orders are difficult to execute. The AON bid or offer cannot be announced in the trading crowd because someone might hit just part of the order, an event that would not be acceptable to the client.

Fill or Kill (FOK)

Fill or kill is a variation on the all-or-none order. It dictates that the entire trade must be done at one time, and additionally that the trade, if executed, must be done right away. An order to sell 25,000 IBM @ 106.00 FOK (fill or kill) is entered. As with the AON order, it cannot be announced in the trading crowd, and the attempt to sell the entire 25,000-share block must be made right away. If the trade cannot be made immediately, it is canceled. The client will get a response very quickly after the order is entered—either a report on the entire 25,000 shares (no partial executions accepted) or a "nothing done." An FOK is very similar to an AON, except that the latter may be executed at any time during the trading day while the former must be executed (or canceled) right away.

Immediate or Cancel (IOC)

An immediate-or-cancel instruction, like the fill-or-kill, limits the time in which the buy or sell attempt is to be made to just a few moments. Unlike either an all-or-none or a fill-or-kill order, the client will accept a partial execution. An order to buy 15,000 FGD @ 29.00 IOC means "buy as many shares of FGD as you can, up to 15,000 shares, at 29.00 or better and cancel the rest—and do it right away." The client will receive a quick response—either a report that some or all of the stock was purchased and the balance canceled, or "nothing done."

Not Held (NH)

A not-held order gives discretion to the floor broker to use his or her own judgment as to the timing or pricing of a block order. The customer is saying, in effect, "I want to buy (or sell) such and such a block of stock. Use your judgment as to how and when to do the trade. If I ultimately pay more than the current market price for the purchase, or receive less than the current market price on the sale, I won't hold you responsible." Specialists are not permitted to handle not-held orders.

Market on Close

The market-on-close order instructs the floor broker to execute a buy or sell order within the last minute or so of the trading day. The order will not necessarily be executed at the last trading price of the day. This type of instruction may be added to a limit order. The customer might be trying to hit a certain price during the trading day, but if the limit order can't be executed, he wants it changed to a market-on-close order so he is assured of a same-day execution.

TIME IN FORCE

If no specific time limit is written on an order, it is assumed to be a *day order*. Day orders remain in force for the balance of the trading day on which they are entered, that is, until the market closes that same day. If the client wants the order to continue to remain in effect, the order is placed as a *good-till-canceled* (GTC) *order*. GTC orders (also known as *open orders*) remain in effect until they are executed or until the client cancels the order. The client may enter such time designations as *good the week* (the orders remain in effect until the close of business on the last trading day of the week during which they are entered), or *good the month*, or good through a specific date such as *good through July 20.* While clients have a great deal of latitude with respect to the time they wish their open orders to remain in force, specialists accept only day or GTC orders from commission-house brokers. Should a client enter a good-the-week order, the brokerage house will enter it as a GTC order with the specialist, and then has the responsibility to cancel that order with the specialist after the close of business on Friday if the order has not been executed by that time.

SUMMARY

The major types of orders are market, limit, stop, and stop limit. Market orders are executed quickly, at the best available price at the time they reach the trading area. Limit orders may be executed if the limit price is reached. Stop orders become market orders when the stop price is reached or breached, and stop limit orders become limit orders when the stop price is reached or breached. Many limit and stop orders are never executed. The limit or stop prices may be changed (either once or several times) or the orders may be canceled before the limit or stop prices are reached.

Stop orders may be used as a type of hedge, affording automatic order entry when and if certain price levels are attained. Stop orders can be utilized to prevent runaway losses or to protect an already-established profit.

Limit orders to sell, buy stop orders, and buy stop limit orders are entered *above* the market; limit orders to buy, sell stop orders, and sell stop limit orders are entered *below* the market.

Unless otherwise specified, all orders are day orders and remain in effect only until the market closes on the day the orders are entered.

MULTIPLE-CHOICE QUIZ

Which type of order would be most appropriate in each of the following situations?

1. Client wants to protect most of his profit on a long position, but wants to stay long in the event the stock goes higher.
    a. buy stop
    b. buy limit
    c. sell stop
    d. sell limit

2. An investor believes her stock will sell two points higher than the present price and wishes to sell if it gets to that level.
    a. market
    b. limit
    c. stop
    d. stop limit

3. An investor wishes to close out a position because he believes the security has peaked pricewise.
    a. market
    b. limit
    c. stop
    d. stop limit

4. An investor wants to limit her loss on a short position, but does not want to receive a price that is dramatically above the electing trade.
    a. market
    b. limit
    c. stop
    d. stop limit

5. An investor wishes to sell 100 shares of NMV that he has owned for quite some time. He wants to sell at about current market levels, but wishes the floor broker executing the order to use her discretion as to the exact timing and pricing of the execution.
    a. all or none
    b. immediate or cancel
    c. not held
    d. fill or kill

PRACTICE EXERCISES

TRUE or FALSE

1. A limit order to buy is entered below the market.

2. A buy stop order is entered above the market.

3. A day order remains in effect for 24 hours after it is entered.

4. Limit orders are always executed if the market is open.

5. If no specific time limit is written on an order, it is assumed to be a day order.

6. GTC orders remain in effect until the stock goes ex-dividend.

7. A sell stop order becomes a limit order when the stop price is reached or breached.

8. To protect an already-established profit on a long position, a client might enter a sell stop order.

9. To protect against a runaway loss on a newly established short position, a client might enter a buy stop order.

10. A stop limit order has a better chance at execution than a stop order.

11. A not-held order indicates that the specialist has been given discretion to use his or her own judgment.

MULTIPLE-CHOICE ANSWERS AND EXPLANATIONS

1. **c.** stop order

    This is a classic use of the stop order. An investor enjoying a 20-point profit might enter a sell stop 2 points or so under the current market and thus preserve approximately 18 points of his profit while still remaining long and able to participate in further gains.

2. **b.** limit order

    The customer has a strong opinion about the future course of the price and is willing to take the chance that the stock will sell at that level. She must appreciate that, if she is wrong, she may ultimately sell the stock for less than the limit price, possibly even for less than the current market price. That's the fatal flaw with all limit orders—you may not get an execution. Is a bird in the hand worth two in the bush?

3. **a.** market order

    This is the best type of order to enter when you are satisfied with the current market level. It's clean and quick.

4. **d.** stop limit

    The client wants to limit her loss exposure on a short position, but doesn't want to cover the short at a runaway price. If she is short at 95.00 and enters an order to "buy 100 VCX @ 98.00 stop, 98.25 limit," there will not be a problem if the stock trades at 96.00, 96.50, 97.00, 97.50, 98.00, or 98.10. Her stop-limit order will be elected by the first trade at 98.00 and her limit order to buy will be executed on the next tick, at 98.10. The danger is that the trades after the 98.00 trade might be 99.00, 99.50, 100.00, and so on. In this event, the customer will not be able to cover her short. Entering a stop-limit instruction therefore might turn out to be false security.

5. **c.** not held

    The other three choices are utilized primarily by institutions trading very large blocks of stock. "Not held" indicates that the client will not hold the broker responsible if he ultimately pays more on a purchase or receives less on a sale than the market price at the time the order was entered.

ANSWERS TO PRACTICE EXERCISES

1. TRUE Limit orders to buy are entered below the market, as the client is attempting to purchase at less than the current market price.

2. TRUE Buy stops are entered above the market; sell stops are entered below the market.

3. FALSE Day orders expire at the end of the trading day on which they are entered.

4. FALSE Many limit orders are never executed.

5. TRUE Lacking any time instruction, orders are considered day orders.

6. FALSE They remain in effect despite the ex-dividend date.

7. FALSE Buy stops and sell stops become market orders when their stop prices are reached or breached.

8. TRUE This automatically sells the stock if it declines.

9. TRUE This automatically covers the short position if it rises in price.

10. FALSE Limit orders might never be executed.

11. FALSE Specialists cannot accept not-held orders.

CHAPTER 18

Short Sales

Most texts define a *short sale* as "selling something you don't own." That is sometimes true, but not always. We define a short sale as *a sale in which delivery is made with borrowed securities*. That's what makes a sale a short sale—delivering securities that have been borrowed. Let's look at the mechanics.

EXECUTING A SHORT SALE

Joseph Kucz is bearish on Marion Corporation (MBB) and thinks it will decline in price. He instructs his broker (Greenberg & Walden) to sell short 1,000 shares of Marion at the current market price of $98 per share. Joe's broker borrows 1,000 shares of Marion from one of its margin customers (Lori Carlos) and delivers the borrowed shares to the buying broker, Mickey & Co. Since Joe was flat at the time of sale, he is now *short* 1,000 shares of MBB and someday must return those borrowed shares. Mickey & Co. is not aware that the shares it purchased at 98 were sold short, and does not need to know. Mickey & Co. bought 1,000 shares of MBB at 98—paid the money and received the shares—and is not concerned with where the selling broker got the shares from.

Short sales may be effected for investors who are flat, long, or short. It's not the investor's beginning position that makes a sale a short sale; it's the fact that the sale is finalized by the delivery of borrowed securities.

CLOSING OUT THE SHORT TRANSACTION

Mr. Kucz was correct in his assumption that Marion would decline, because shortly after he sold MBB short the shares declined in price to 82 per share. Joe then *bought* 1,000 shares at that price to cover the short sale. This made

Joe flat again, as the covering buy canceled the short position. Joe sold (short) 1,000 shares at 98 and bought them back at 82, for an overall gross profit of $16,000. After Joe covered the short position, his broker returned the borrowed shares to Lori Carlos' account. It's a very interesting transaction—first you sell and then you buy. The trick is to sell at a high price and then buy back later at a lower price.

In most instances the client from whom the shares are borrowed (Lori Carlos in our example) is unaware of the fact. Mrs. Carlos' account is not at risk because the borrowing broker (Greenberg & Walden) ensures that there is always sufficient cash on hand to repurchase the borrowed shares and thus restore her position. In the interim, Mrs. Carlos' account continues to show her long 1,000 shares of MBB. There is no indication on her monthly statement when the shares are borrowed or when they are returned. Lori continues to receive any dividends due her and is free to sell her MBB at any time.

MARKING TO THE MARKET

Until Mrs. Carlos' 1,000 shares are returned, it is the responsibility of Greenberg & Walden to see to it that they have sufficient cash on hand to repurchase the shares. This amount is *marked-to-the-market* daily. The initial required collateral was $98,000 (1,000 shares at 98). If the borrowed shares were to rise in value to 102, then the required collateral would be $102,000 (1,000 shares at 102) and the difference between the initial collateral ($98,000) and the currently required collateral, or $4,000, would be charged to Mr. Kucz's account and added to the amount escrowed for Mrs. Carlos' account. If MBB were then to decline in value to 90, the required collateral would be only $90,000 and Mr. Kucz's account would be credited with $12,000 ($102,000 − $90,000), reducing the escrow for Mrs. Carlos. This mark-to-the-market is recalculated each trading day, with Joe's account debited when the price of MBB rises and credited if the price of MBB declines.

THE RISKS AND REWARDS OF SHORT SELLING

When Joe Kucz sold 1,000 shares of MBB short at 98, he was expecting MBB to decline in price—he was bearish on the stock and wanted to buy it back (to cover) at a lower price. His plan was to sell high, and then to buy low. What was his maximum profit potential? The most he could have made on the trade was $98,000 (less expenses). If MBB went bankrupt—down to zero—then Joe would effectively have sold for $98,000 and bought back (covered) for zero, making a profit of $98,000. The highest profit anyone can make on a short sale is the difference between the short sale price and zero.

But what if Joe was wrong in his opinion and, instead of going down, MBB rose in price? As MBB goes higher and higher, Joe's broker (Greenberg & Walden) will ask him to deposit more and more money to cover the marks-to-the-market. If Joe is willing and able to meet all these maintenance calls (described in Chapter 19), he can continue to maintain his short position and hope that ultimately MBB will decline to a price below 98. If he cannot or will not meet these demands for additional capital, then his broker will buy him in, closing out the short position. At least in theory, there is no limit to the amount Joe might lose, because there is no upper limit as to how high a stock can rise in price. That's the downside to short selling—there is a limit to how much you can make, but *no* limit to how much you can lose.

Another negative to a short position has to do with dividends. If MBB pays a dividend while Joe Kucz is short, then Joe will be *charged* with the dividend. Since Mrs. Carlos owns 1,000 shares of MBB that have been taken from her account to cover the short sale, her dividend must come from Mr. Kucz. All the while that Joe is short, he will be paying out any dividends that are declared on his short position. When you are long a stock, you may be receiving dividends, but while you are short a stock you may be paying out dividends.

Still another negative to short selling is that a successful short transaction can never result in a long-term gain. All short-sale profits are short-term gains, regardless of the length of time the short position has been held open. Short-sale profits are thus always subject to the maximum tax, and the short seller can never take advantage of the relatively light tax treatment given to long-term profits.

Short selling is a sophisticated strategy that the average investor rarely utilizes. The possibility of unlimited loss, the negative cash flow (dividends charged against the short seller), and the unavailability of long-term gains make short selling too risky a proposition for any but the most experienced traders.

THE TICK RULE

Every stock trade has a *tick*. If a stock goes up in price, that higher price is a plus tick. Should a stock trade first at 45.00 and then at 45.10, that second trade (45.10) is a plus tick, also known as an uptick. If the next trade is at 45.15, that too is an uptick. If a stock's price goes down, say from 67.75 to 67.70, the second trade is a minus tick (downtick). In the following sequence of trades—23.50, 23.55, 23.60, 23.55, 23.50—the second, third, fourth, and fifth trades are, respectively, plus tick, plus tick, minus tick, minus tick.

When a stock's price doesn't change between trades, the last sale is a zero tick—either a zero-plus tick or a zero-minus tick depending upon whether the previous tick was a plus or a minus. Examples: A stock trades at 43.10, then at 43.15. The second trade is an uptick. The next trade is also at 43.15. This trade is a zero-plus tick, as the price didn't change and the previous tick was a plus. If it trades yet again at 43.15, that trade is also a zero-plus tick. If a stock trades at 32.65 and then at 32.60, the second trade is a minus tick. Should the stock again trade at 32.60, that will be a zero-minus tick, as the price didn't change and the previous tick was a minus.

Every trade, therefore, is either a plus tick, a zero-plus tick, a minus tick, or a zero-minus tick. The tick carries over from day to day. If a stock closes at 105.65 on a given day, on a plus tick, and opens the following day at 105.75, that opening trade is a plus tick. If it had opened at 105.60, that would be a minus tick, and if it opened at 105.65, that would be a zero-plus tick. Short sales on stock exchanges may be made only on *plus* or *zero-plus* ticks. It is the responsibility of the broker handling the short sale order to make sure that the tick rule is observed. The buying broker needn't be concerned with the tick. He or she simply agrees to pay for the stock at the trade price and has no knowledge (or interest) as to whether the delivery of the shares will be made with borrowed stock.

If a broker with a market order to sell short an exchange-listed security enters the trading crowd and notes that the previous trade was at 93.50, a plus tick, then she can attempt to sell short at 93.50 or higher, as that price represents a plus or a zero-plus tick. She could not attempt to sell short at 93.49 or lower, because such a trade would create a minus tick. That's one of the reasons that quotation devices indicate the tick (either + or –); it serves as a guide to the short-selling broker.

The Nasdaq Short Sale Rule prohibits NASD members from selling a Nasdaq National Market stock at or below the inside best bid, when that price is lower than the previous inside best bid in that stock. The Nasdaq rule essentially follows the NYSE rule, using the inside bid rather than the last sale.

The New York and American Stock Exchanges and the Nasdaq Stock Market regularly report the short positions in their securities. These reports are carried in the financial press monthly and are followed closely by market technicians. The reports highlight dramatic changes, either plus or minus, in previously reported short positions, and also indicate those instances in which short positions might be due to an arbitrage.

REASONS FOR SELLING SHORT

There are many reasons for selling short. One reason is to attempt to profit from a decline in price, but short sales have many other applications. A short sale may be used as a hedge against a long position. If an individual or institution is concerned that one of its large long positions might decline in value, it may utilize a short sale in an equivalent security as a form of insurance. The theory is that if the long position goes down in price, the offsetting short position will also decline. The loss on the long position will thus be balanced by a corresponding profit on the short position. The investor could, of course, simply sell the long position, eliminating it from the portfolio, but that would put it out of the market and unable to profit from a rise in the security's price. By selling short an equivalent security, the investor remains long the original stock and avoids the tax consequences of an outright sale. If both securities remain stable in price, the short position can be covered when the client believes the crisis is over.

SUMMARY

A short sale is settled by the delivery of borrowed securities. Any security that can be borrowed can be sold short, even U.S. government securities. The commonest reason for selling short is to attempt to profit from a decline in a security's price—first to sell short at a high price, and then to buy back (cover) at a lower price. Those with a bearish outlook thus hope to profit if a security declines in value. In theory, there is a cap on the amount one can make from a short sale—the difference between the sale price and zero—but no limit on the amount one can lose. A stock can go no lower than zero, but there is no limit to how high it can go.

Short sales can be effected only on plus ticks or zero-plus ticks. Short sales can be made only in margin accounts, and the short seller must deposit at least 50% of the value of the stock sold short. The short seller is also charged for any dividends paid on the borrowed shares, and may be called upon to deposit additional monies if the short security goes up in price.

MULTIPLE-CHOICE QUIZ

1. What is the maximum profit potential for an investor shorting 100 shares at 36?

   a. $1,800
   b. $3,600
   c. unlimited
   d. cannot be determined

2. What is the maximum loss potential for an investor shorting 200 shares at 106?

   a. $10,600
   b. $21,200
   c. unlimited
   d. cannot be determined

3. On which sequence of trades might a short sale be executed? (The first trade in each sequence is a zero-minus tick.)

   a. 23.25—23.25—23.20
   b. 35.50—35.55—35.60
   c. 98.00—97.95—97.95
   d. 106.75—106.75—106.65

4. When must borrowed securities be returned to the lender?

   a. within one month of the short sale
   b. within one year of the short sale
   c. when the short security declares a dividend
   d. there is no particular time limit

5. A short sale may be effected by an investor who is _____ at the time of the short sale.

   I long
   II short
   III flat

   a. I only
   b. III only
   c. I or II only
   d. I, II, or III

PRACTICE EXERCISES

1. The first trade in the following sequence is a *plus* tick. Identify each of the 5 subsequent ticks.

    45.15   45.15   45.15   45.10   45.05   45.05

2. The first trade in the following sequence is a *minus* tick. Identify each of the five subsequent ticks.

    12.05   12.00   12.00   12.05   12.10   12.10

3. The first trade in the following sequence is a *zero-plus* tick. Identify each of the five subsequent ticks.

    88.00   87.95   88.00   88.05   88.10   88.00

4. The first trade in the following sequence is a *zero-minus* tick. Identify each of the five subsequent ticks.

    9.05   9.05   9.00   8.95   9.00   9.05

5. The first trade in the following sequence is a *minus* tick. On which of the five subsequent trades could a short sale have been executed?

    19.95   19.95   20.00   20.00   19.95   19.95

An investor wants to sell 100 NFW short, if and when it declines to 119.00 from its current price of 124.50. She is not concerned with selling short at exactly 119.00, but does want to sell short at the best then-prevailing price, if and when NFW trades at 119.00 or lower.

6. What order might she enter?

7. What constraints, if any, are on the broker handling the short sale order on the NYSE floor?

8. When will the short sale be executed?

9. What price is guaranteed to the short seller?

10. If the short sale is executed, what is the short seller's maximum potential profit?

11. If the short sale is executed, what is the short seller's maximum potential loss?

12. If the short sale is executed, when will the short seller have to cover?

13. What is the source of the shares to be sold short?

14. If the short sale is executed, what type of order might the short seller enter if she wishes to hedge her position?

XYZ closes on April 13 at 78.85. The stock trades ex an $0.80 cash dividend the following day (April 14) and closes at 78.00.

15. What is the stock's net change for the day?

ABC's last three trades on November 2 are, in order, 26.35, 26.40, and 26.35. The stock trades ex a $0.15 dividend the following day, November 3. Its first three trades on that day are 26.20, 26.20, and 26.15. Its closing price on November 3 is 26.

16. What type of tick is each of the first three trades?

17. What is ABC's net change for November 3?

DEF closes at 108.75 (a minus tick) and begins to trade the following day ex a dividend of $1.05.

18. What is the lowest price at which stock can be offered for a short sale at the opening on that day?

You are bearish on Pinder Corporation and wish to sell 1,000 shares short at its current market price of 98.50. Pinder Corporation 105 calls are trading at 3.25. If you sold 1,000 shares short, without hedging:

19. What would be your maximum profit potential?

20. What would be your maximum loss potential?

21. How would you hedge your short position using the 105 calls, and what would be the dollar cost of the hedge?

22. With the position hedged, what would be your maximum profit potential?

23. With the position hedged, what would be your maximum loss potential?

24. Could you also hedge the short position by buying Pinder Corporation puts or by selling Pinder Corporation calls?

MULTIPLE-CHOICE ANSWERS AND EXPLANATIONS

1. **b.** The stock can only go down to zero. If it does (however unlikely), the client will have sold for $3,600 and bought back for zero, making a profit of $3,600.

2. **c.** With any short sale, there is no limit to how much the short seller might lose because there is no upper limit (at least in theory) on a security's price.

3. **b.** Only sequence b contains an uptick—in fact, there are two upticks (both the second and third trades). The second and third trades in the other sequences are: a—zero-minus, minus; c—minus, zero-minus; d—zero-minus, minus.

4. **d.** There is no specific time limit. As long as the short seller meets demands for additional collateral if the short stock rises in price, he or she can stay short for an indefinite period.

5. **d.** An investor can be long, short, or flat when he or she executes a short sale. The delivery of borrowed securities is what makes it a short sale, not the client's position before the trade.

ANSWERS TO PRACTICE EXERCISES

1. Zero-plus, zero-plus, minus, minus, zero-minus

2. Minus, zero-minus, plus, plus, zero-plus

3. Minus, plus, plus, plus, minus

4. Zero-minus, minus, minus, plus, plus

5. Short sales could have been executed only on two of the trades: the first trade at 20.00 (a plus tick), and the second trade at 20.00 (a zero-plus tick). The other three trades at 19.95 (after the initial trade) are, in order, zero-minus, minus, and zero-minus, and thus ineligible for a short sale.

6. Sell short 100 NFW at 119.00 stop.

   This memorandum to the specialist requests that an order to sell 100 NFW short be entered just after the first trade in NFW at or below 119.00.

7. The short sale can be executed only on a plus tick or a zero-plus tick.

   It is the selling broker's responsibility to ensure that the short sale is executed in conformance with the tick rule.

8. The trade will be done on the first uptick after the electing trade at or below 119.00.

   If there are no upticks (the stock is falling precipitously), there will be no occasion to execute the short sale.

9. No particular price is guaranteed.

   The trade might be executed at a price considerably lower than 119.00.

10. The maximum potential profit is the amount of the short sale.

    If the stock is shorted at 119.00, the investor's profit potential is $11,900. In theory, she could cover for zero if the stock went bankrupt.

11. Unlimited

    As with all unhedged short positions, the loss exposure is unlimited.

12. There is no specific time limitation.

    So long as the client is willing and able to satisfy any demands for additional collateral that the carrying broker might require, the client may remain short as long as she wants.

13. The firm carrying her account will arrange to borrow the shares.

    The shares might come from a variety of sources including the brokerage's proprietary holdings, one of its margin customers, or another brokerage.

14. A buy stop order

    Having sold short at 119.00 or so, she might enter a buy stop at 125.00, which would limit her loss to about 6 points.

15. Down $0.05

    The 78.85 closing price must be adjusted downward to 78.05 to account for the $0.80 dividend. Comparing the adjusted closing price on April 13 (78.05) with the closing price on April 14 (78.00) gives a net change of "down $0.05."

16. Zero-minus, zero-minus, and minus

    The final trade on November 2 was 26.35, a minus tick. This price must be adjusted downward to 26.20 to account for the $0.15 dividend. When the stock opens on November 3 at 26.20, it is considered unchanged from the previous day's *adjusted* close of 26.20, so that first trade is a zero-minus tick. The next trade, at 26.20, is also a zero-minus tick. The next trade, at 26.15, is a minus tick.

17. Down $0.20

    The stock's net change for the day would be "down 20" as the closing price of 26.00 on November 3 would be compared with the *adjusted* closing price of 26.20 on November 2.

18. 107.71

    The closing price of 108.75 must be adjusted downward to 107.70 to reflect the $1.05 dividend that the stock no longer carries. Since 108.75 was a minus tick, an opening the next day at 107.70 would be considered unchanged, and a zero-minus tick. Since short sales can be effected only on a plus or zero-plus tick, the stock can be offered only at 107.71 (or higher), which would be an uptick.

19. $98,500

You only benefit from a decline in the price of the shorted stock. A stock can go down only to zero. If it does become worthless, you can buy (cover) for zero something you sold at 98.50, thus making that many points on the 1,000 shares ($98.50 × 1,000 = $98,500).

20. Unlimited

As there is no limit to how high the stock might trade, there is no limit (at least in theory) to how much you might lose.

21. One would hedge by buying 10 Pinder Corp. calls; the cost of the hedge would be $3,250.

Purchasing 10 calls gives the short seller the right to buy 1,000 shares of stock at 105 per share. With each call trading at 3.25 ($325), the cost of 10 such calls would be $3,250.

22. $95,250

The calls cost $3,250, and this reduces the maximum profit potential by the same amount. It's the insurance cost. $98,500 − $3,250 = $95,250

23. $9,750

If the stock goes up, the worst the short seller can do (during the life of the calls) is to buy back at 105, limiting your trading loss to 6.50 points per share, or $6,500. Remember to factor in the cost of the calls ($3,250), which will give you an overall loss exposure of $9,750.

24. No

Buying puts would be of value if the stock went down. The short position would be profitable, and additional money would be made on the long puts, but it would not constitute a hedge. Selling calls would bring in additional profit if the stock went down, similar to buying puts; while this would generate additional profit, it also would not be a hedge. Buying calls would be a *partial* hedge because it brings in only the premiums written, small consolation if the stock goes way up and the investor loses a great amount on the short position.

CHAPTER 19

Margin Trading

CASH ACCOUNTS AND MARGIN ACCOUNTS

The majority of investors trade on a cash basis. They pay in full for the securities they purchase, and are then free either to leave those securities in their brokers' care (in street name) or to take delivery of them. "Pay as you go" accounts are known as *cash accounts*. Once payment is made, the client has no further financial obligations, and the brokerage firm is not at risk in any way since it did not extend the client any credit. It's like buying an automobile for cash—there's no car loan, and therefore no obligation to pay interest to a lender or to give a lender the right to repossess the car. The car is yours, free and clear.

Another type of account is known as a *margin account*. In this type of account the client pays only a portion of the purchase price and borrows the remainder from the brokerage firm. The client's securities must remain with the brokerage firm, in street name, as they are the security for the loan extended by the broker. When you take out a car loan, you pay only a portion of the purchase price and borrow the balance from a lender (bank or auto manufacturer). The lending organization will hold the car's title papers until the loan is repaid in full; then the title is given to the car owner. The car is the collateral for the loan. If the borrower fails to meet the obligation to repay the principal and interest, the lender can repossess the car. Similarly, in a margin account, the brokerage firm has the right to sell some or all of the margin customer's securities if the investor fails to meet additional requests for funds (maintenance calls).

REASONS FOR TRADING ON MARGIN

Investors utilize margin accounts to employ *leverage*. For the same amount of money, one can purchase double the number of shares in a margin account as opposed to a cash account. The good news is that any profits are effectively doubled: For a given amount of money, investors will make twice as much profit trading on margin as they would trading on a cash basis, giving them more "bang for the buck." The bad news is that trading a given dollar amount on a margin basis also results in the doubling of any *losses* as compared with a cash account. Twice the profit potential—and twice the risk.

Many securities can be bought on margin—virtually every exchange-listed security and many thousands of OTC securities, as well as corporate, government, and municipal bonds. Certain transactions can be effected *only* in margin accounts. These include the sale (writing) of options (the purchase of options must be for cash) and short sales.

REGULATION T

The Federal Reserve sets the minimum "down payment" that one must deposit when purchasing stocks on margin. The rate has varied widely over time, but has been set at 50% for many years. An investor who buys (or sells short) stocks on margin must deposit a minimum of 50% of the purchase price. This minimum amount is known as the *Reg. T requirement*.

Note: Reg. T requirements vary for different types of securities (stocks, options, nonconvertible bonds, convertible bonds, etc.). This text is concerned only with the requirements for *stock* transactions.

The investor can elect to deposit more than the Reg. T requirement (currently 50%), but must deposit at least that amount. The broker's notification to a client that a deposit is required against the purchase of securities in a margin account is known as a *Reg. T call*, sometimes also called a margin call, a Federal call, or simply the initial requirement.

Mrs. Mary Lou Rapp purchases 1,000 shares of XYZ at 56.00 per share in a newly opened margin account. The purchase is valued at $56,000 (excluding commissions), and Mrs. Rapp will receive a T call for 50% of that amount, or $28,000. Assuming that Mrs. Rapp sends in the exact amount of the call, this is what her account will look like after her check for $28,000 is deposited:

Long Market Value	$56,000	(the value of the stock in the account)
Debit Balance	−28,000	(the amount Mrs. Rapp owes the broker)
Equity	$28,000	(Mrs. Rapp's equity [net worth] in the account)

Note that Mary Lou's "mortgage" is for $28,000. She put up 50% of the purchase price and her broker put up the other 50%, so she owes the broker

$28,000, her *debit balance*. Her equity represents the amount of money she would receive were the account to be liquidated and the broker's loan repaid. The long market value represents her *assets*, the debit balance represents her *liabilities*, and the equity represents her *net worth*. That's the basic margin account equation: total assets minus total liabilities equals net worth.

REQUIRED PAPERS

Opening a margin account is slightly more complicated than opening a cash account. Several additional forms have to be signed, including a margin agreement (also known as a customers' agreement), to demonstrate that the margin client is aware of three important points:

1. The margin account client cannot take delivery of his or her securities. They must remain in street name with the broker, as collateral for the client's debit balance.

2. The client will be charged interest on his or her debit balance. It is, after all, a loan, and as such is subject to interest charges.

3. If the equity in the account falls below certain levels, the client must deposit additional cash or additional collateral, or be subject to a sell-out.

These are important considerations that apply only to margin accounts, not to cash accounts. The client must be aware of the additional risk he or she is assuming by trading on margin rather than for cash. Having the client acknowledge these points is quite important to the brokerage firm; it must be able to demonstrate that the client is aware of the risks, restrictions, and interest charges applicable to margin accounts.

WHEN THE STOCKS IN A MARGIN ACCOUNT INCREASE IN PRICE

Let's follow Mrs. Rapp's new margin account. If the stock she bought (1,000 shares of XYZ @ 56.00) rises in value to a per-share price of 72.00, then her account will look like this:

Long Market Value	$72,000	(the value of the stock in the account)
Debit Balance	−28,000	(the amount Mrs. Rapp owes the broker)
Equity	$44,000	(Mrs. Rapp's equity [net worth] in the account)

Mrs. Rapp's long market value is now $72,000 (1,000 shares at 72.00 per share), but she still owes the original $28,000 that was loaned to her to help pay for the stock, so her debit balance is unchanged at $28,000, but her equity is now $44,000. Her stock went up in value, her debit balance remained unchanged, so her equity increased. The broker will note this increase in Mary Lou's fortunes and will make a note that her account now has a Special Memorandum Account (SMA) balance of $8,000.

THE SPECIAL MEMORANDUM ACCOUNT (SMA)

Here's how Mary Lou's SMA was figured: Her new equity ($44,000) was compared with her new long market value ($72,000). The new market value has an initial requirement of $36,000 (50% of $72,000), but the account now has equity of $44,000. The amount by which the new equity exceeds the new initial requirement is known as excess equity or SMA: $44,000 − $36,000 = $8,000. The SMA gives Mary Lou some options with her margin account: She may ask her broker to send her a check for any amount up to the SMA ($8,000), or she may buy as much as an additional $16,000 worth of additional securities without putting up any more money, or she can do nothing at present, reserving the first two options for a later time.

Using the SMA—Cash Withdrawal

Should Mary Lou wish to increase her debit balance now that she has a "line of credit" of $8,000, here's what her account would look like both before and after the $8,000 check was sent to her.

	Before	**After**
Long Market Value	$72,000	$72,000
Debit Balance	−28,000	−36,000
Equity	$44,000	$36,000
SMA	$ 8,000	0

When the broker sent Mrs. Rapp a check for $8,000, that increased her debit balance by the same amount, from $28,000 to $36,000. Her equity was thus reduced to $36,000 and her SMA, having been "used," is now zero. Note that her new equity ($36,000) is now exactly 50% of her new long market value ($72,000).

Using the SMA—Buying Additional Securities

Mrs. Rapp's SMA might be used instead to purchase additional securities without having to deposit additional cash. The dollar amount of the purchase is known as her "buying power." Her buying power is calculated by multiplying her SMA by two. Her SMA of $8,000 translates to a buying power of $16,000 ($8,000 × 2). If Mary Lou chose to utilize her SMA by buying an additional $16,000 worth of securities, here's what her account would look like both before and after the new purchase.

	Before	**After**
Long Market Value	$72,000	$88,000
Debit Balance	−28,000	−44,000
Equity	$44,000	$44,000
SMA	$ 8,000	0

Note that Mary Lou bought an additional $16,000 worth of stock, which increased her long market value by that amount, making the new market value $88,000. Since she didn't put up any additional funds, her broker paid the entire amount of the new purchase ($16,000), which increased Mary Lou's debit balance by that amount, to $44,000. Her equity remains at $44,000 (50% of the new market value) and her SMA has been "used," reducing it to zero.

We have shown how Mrs. Rapp might have used her SMA either to withdraw cash or to buy additional securities, but remember that she might have done nothing. There was no need for her to take either step at the first opportunity. Interestingly, her SMA (and buying power) would *not* be reduced if her market value were to fall at a later date. Had she not utilized her SMA and her stock retreated to her original price of 56.00, her account would have been back to this structure:

Long Market Value	$56,000
Debit Balance	−28,000
Equity	$28,000

However, she would still have an SMA of $8,000 and buying power of $16,000. This is a unique feature of SMA—it doesn't go down until and unless it is used.

MAINTENANCE REQUIREMENTS

The Federal Reserve is involved with margin accounts only insofar as the required down payment is concerned. Once the Reg. T call has been satisfied, the Federal Reserve is out of the picture. Several other parties are interested in the account on a continuing basis, however, including the stock exchanges, the NASD, and the brokerage firms. After the initial requirement has been satisfied, these other parties ensure that margin accounts are monitored on a continuing basis. When an account's equity has declined below the carrying broker's minimum maintenance requirements, that firm will issue a *maintenance call*. This is a request that the client deposit additional funds (or collateral) to bring the account up to its minimum standards. Brokerage firms are free to set their own minimum maintenance requirements, but they must be at least as high as the "industry standard" set by the NYSE and the NASD. The standard minimum requirement is currently 25%. Most brokerage houses have a "house" requirement of 30% or 35%.

Using the industry's most lenient maintenance requirement (25%), here's an example of a margin account requiring a maintenance call:

Long Market Value	$60,000
Debit Balance	−48,000
Equity	$12,000 (20% of market value)

Note that the maintenance requirement for this account is $15,000 (25% of the $60,000 market value). Since the account's equity is only $12,000, it is $3,000 under the 25% equity minimum. Therefore, a maintenance call for $3,000 will be issued.

MEETING A MAINTENANCE CALL

Should the market not bounce back, thus increasing the account's market value and equity to the required minimum, there are three methods for satisfying the $3,000 maintenance call: depositing cash, depositing additional collateral, or liquidation (selling out).

Cash Deposit

The maintenance call can be met by the client depositing cash in the amount of the call, $3,000. After the client sends in the funds, the account will be structured this way:

Long Market Value	$60,000
Debit Balance	−45,000
Equity	$15,000 (25% of market value)

The deposit of $3,000 cash decreased the debit balance by that amount and increased the equity by the same amount. Note that the account's equity is now exactly 25% of its market value

Deposit of Additional Collateral

The client may also meet the maintenance call by depositing additional fully-paid-for securities rather than cash. To meet a call in this manner, however, the client must deposit additional securities with a value equal to *133% of the amount of the call*. The $3,000 call thus requires a collateral deposit of $4,000 (133% of $3,000). After the customer sends in the additional securities with a market value of $4,000, the account will look this way:

Long Market Value	$64,000
Debit Balance	−48,000
Equity	$16,000 (25% of market value)

The market value increased by the amount of the securities deposited, the debit balance remained the same, and the equity increased to $16,000, exactly 25% of the account's new market value.

Liquidation

If the client is unable or unwilling to meet the maintenance call through the deposit of cash or additional collateral, the only remaining alternative is to "sell out." For a maintenance call to be satisfied through liquidation, securities in the account worth *four times the amount of the call* must be sold. To meet the $3,000 maintenance call, the client would have to sell $12,000 worth of securities in the account (4 × $3,000). After the sale, the account would have this appearance:

Long Market Value	$48,000
Debit Balance	−36,000
Equity	$12,000 (25% of market value)

Note that the $12,000 sale decreased the long market value by that amount and decreased the debit balance by the same amount. The account's equity is now exactly 25% of the new market value.

HOW LOW CAN IT GO?

Margin clients are understandably concerned about the possibility of receiving a maintenance call. A natural question is, "When will my account be in jeopardy?" To determine a margin account's *lowest permissible market value* before receiving a maintenance call (given a 25% maintenance requirement), simply multiply the account's debit balance by $4/3$. Example: Frank Berretta has a margin account with the following structure:

Long Market Value	$120,000
Debit Balance	− 30,000
Equity	$ 90,000

Mr. Berretta's account is in excellent shape. In fact, Frank has an SMA of at least $30,000 and at least $60,000 in buying power. But Frank is a worrier by nature, and he wants to know when he might receive a maintenance call. Telling him that he will receive such a call if and when his equity declines to less than 25% of his then-current market value doesn't convey much information—in fact, it's confusing. Multiplying the debit balance in Frank's account by $4/3$ gives us the exact information: $30,000 × $4/3$ = $40,000. That's the lowest Frank's market value can decline before he will receive a maintenance call. Let's plug in the numbers to see if it works out.

If the market value of Frank's account goes all the way down from $120,000 to $40,000, this is what his account will look like:

Long Market Value	$40,000

Debit Balance	−30,000
Equity	$10,000 (25% of market value)

Note that Frank's equity will then be exactly 25% of his market value, just above the limit for receiving a maintenance call.

Presuming a 25% maintenance requirement, multiplying a margin account's debit balance by $4/3$ gives the lowest dollar amount to which the account's market value may decline before the account becomes subject to a maintenance call.

SHORT MARGIN ACCOUNTS

The Reg. T requirements are the same for short margin accounts—the short seller must deposit an amount of money equal to at least 50% of the value of the securities sold short. If the securities sold short go *down* in value, SMA and short-selling power are generated; if the short positions go *up* in value, maintenance calls might be issued. Maintenance requirements are set higher for short margin accounts than for long margin accounts, currently at least 30% for high-priced securities and even higher for lower-priced short positions. The purpose of this practice is to discourage the shorting of low-priced stocks. There is very little profit potential (the stock can only go down to zero) but a great deal of risk (there is no limit to how high a stock can rise in price) when one shorts a low-priced stock.

SUMMARY

Margin trading provides leverage, the opportunity to generate greater profits from a given dollar investment than is afforded by dealing in a cash account. However, the risks are also increased, and the client must pay interest on the debit balance in the account. Margin interest is usually greater than the dividends and interest generated by the securities in the account, resulting in a negative cash flow.

The current Reg. T requirement for stocks is 50% for both long and short accounts. The lowest maintenance requirement for long positions is 25% and the lowest maintenance requirement for short positions is 30%. Margin calls are issued when a position is established, long or short. Maintenance calls are issued when the account's equity falls below the minimum requirement. A bear market might result in the issuance of a number of maintenance calls to the holders of long accounts. The financial press often incorrectly refers to these as margin calls.

MULTIPLE-CHOICE QUIZ

Utilize the following information to answer all five questions:

Pauline D. Burwell has a long margin account with a market value of $160,000 and a debit balance of $60,000.

1. What is the equity in Pauline's account?
   a. $60,000
   b. $100,000
   c. $160,000
   d. $220,000

2. What is the SMA in Miss Burwell's account?
   a. zero
   b. $20,000
   c. $40,000
   d. $60,000

3. What is Pauline's buying power?
   a. zero
   b. $20,000
   c. $40,000
   d. $60,000

4. To what market value could Miss Burwell's account fall before she would receive a maintenance call?
   a. $20,000
   b. $40,000
   c. $60,000
   d. $80,000

5. If Pauline utilized her buying power (if any) to the fullest, what would her debit balance be after that trade?
   a. $40,000
   b. $60,000 (unchanged)
   c. $80,000
   d. $100,000

PRACTICE EXERCISES

Ms. Susan Tracey purchases 1,000 shares of NFW at 60.00 in a newly opened margin account.

1. What will be the structure of the account (market value, debit balance, equity) after she meets the Reg. T call?

2. What will be the structure of the account if NFW goes to 80.00?

3. After the move to 80.00, what will be the account's SMA?

4. After the move to 80.00, what will be the account's buying power?

5. To what amount might the account's market value decline before Susan would incur a maintenance call?

MULTIPLE-CHOICE ANSWERS AND EXPLANATIONS

Here's how Pauline Burwell's account is structured:

Long Market Value	$160,000
Debit Balance	−60,000

1. **b.** Subtracting the debit balance from the long market value gives the account's equity: $160,000 (long market value) − $60,000 (debit balance) = $100,000 (equity).

2. **b.** The margin requirement for an account with a market value of $160,000 is 50% of that amount, or $80,000. Pauline's account has equity of $100,000 (see answer to question 1), which is $20,000 in excess of the requirement. This excess is her SMA. Pauline is now able to ask for a check from her broker for any amount up to $20,000. Should she do so, any amount sent to her would increase her debit and decrease her equity; her market value would remain the same.

3. **c.** Pauline's buying power is twice her SMA: $20,000 × 2 = $40,000 buying power. Pauline can now purchase additional securities in any amount up to $40,000 without having to send in additional money. Should she utilize any or all of her buying power, it would increase both her market value and her debit balance; her equity would remain the same.

4. **d.** The lowest permissible market value figure can be arrived at by multiplying the debit balance by $4/3$: $60,000 × $4/3$ = $80,000. We can check our arithmetic by showing the account as it would appear if the market value did go down to that level:

Long Market Value	$80,000	
Debit Balance	−60,000	
Equity	20,000	(25% of market value)

   Note that the account now has equity equal to exactly 25% of the new market value—it's right at the minimum—so we figured correctly.

5. **d.** Buying an additional $40,000 worth of securities (see answer to question 3) would increase Pauline's debit balance by that amount, raising it from $60,000 to $100,000. Keep in mind that someone has to pay for the securities that are bought. If Pauline doesn't send in all the money required for the procedure, then the broker pays for her, thus increasing her debit balance.

ANSWERS TO PRACTICE EXERCISES

1. $60,000 market value – $30,000 debit balance = $30,000 equity

   Susan must deposit 50% of the purchase price, which would leave a debit balance of $30,000, the amount loaned to her by the brokerage.

2. $80,000 market value – $30,000 debit balance = $50,000 equity

   Note that the market value and equity have both increased by the same amount, while the debit balance is unchanged.

3. $10,000

   The required equity for an account with an $80,000 market value is half that amount, or $40,000. Note that the account now has equity of $50,000, which is $10,000 higher than the requirement. This excess equity becomes Susan's SMA.

4. $20,000

   With Reg. T at its current level of 50%, an account's buying power is double its SMA (special memorandum account).

5. $40,000

   The lowest permissible market value before a maintenance call is issued is calculated by multiplying the account's debit balance by $4/3$.

   $$4/3 \times \$30,000 = \$40,000$$

The Analysis of Securities

FUNDAMENTAL ANALYSIS

A company's "books" are generally considered to be its balance sheet and its income statement, and both are carefully scrutinized by analysts and serious investors trying to assess that company's investment possibilities. The study of those statements and other data such as the company's management, marketing, products, sales practices, competition, research and development, and past sales and earnings is known as *fundamental analysis*. Fundamental analysis is undertaken in an effort to forecast companies' future stock-price movements. The other major school of stock analysis is known as *technical analysis*, discussed later in this chapter.

Financial statements show what the company owns, what it owes, the shareholders' equity, how much the company is earning, and how it has been managing its expenses. Think of these statements as the company's report card. A corporation's fortunes can be traced, over time, by an examination of its financial statements. Analysts are concerned with the *trend* of such reports, not merely with the current readings. A student's report card showing all B's would be great news if his former grades had been C's and D's, but bad news if he had always before been a straight-A student.

THE BALANCE SHEET

At regular intervals, corporations prepare a *balance sheet*. This report shows the corporation's assets, liabilities, and net worth. The basic balance sheet equation is: Total Assets − Total Liabilities = Net Worth. What the company owns (assets) minus what it owes (liabilities) is the company's *residual value* (net worth). This is the same formula we used when examining the margin account: Long Market Value (assets) − Debit Balance (liabilities) = Equity (residual value). A simple balance sheet for the Gneiding Corporation is provided.

GNEIDING CORPORATION
BALANCE SHEET—DECEMBER 31, 20XX

Current Assets:		Current Liabilities:	
Cash	$ 1,244,000	Accounts Payable	$ 2,137,000
Marketable Securities	350,000	Accrued Expenses	1,117,000
Accounts Receivable	4,109,000	Accrued Taxes	1,439,000
Inventories	5,006,000	Total Current Liabilities	4,693,00
Total Current Assets	10,709,000		
		Long-Term Liabilities:	
		8% Bonds due 2029	1,250,000
Fixed Assets:		Total Liabilities	5,943,000
Property and Plant	6,385,000		
Equipment	2,663,000	Net Worth:	
Land	3,458,000	7% Preferred Stock	1,235,000
Total Fixed Assets	12,506,000	Common Stock ($1 par)	3,865,000
		Capital Surplus	1,231,000
Intangibles:		Retained Earnings	11,941,000
Goodwill	1,000,000	Total Net Worth	18,272,000
		Total Liabilities	
Total Assets	24,215,000	and Net Worth	24,215,000

Balance Sheet Analysis

Current assets include cash and other items that will become cash in one year or less. We list four such items on our sample balance sheet: cash—bills, coins, and checking account balances; marketable securities—short-term investments (very often T-bills) on which the company can earn a reasonable return on its excess cash; accounts receivable—monies owed to the company by customers who have not yet paid for delivered goods; and inventories—raw materials, partially finished goods, and finished products stockpiled for future sale. The first three of these are considered to be relatively *liquid*; that is, they can quickly be converted to cash. A corporation's cash, marketable securities, and accounts receivable are thus considered to be its *quick assets*. Inventories are relatively illiquid and thus are not included in quick assets.

  Current liabilities are the obligations that the company must honor within the next year—its "budget," if you will. One of the first things an analyst will examine is the relationship between a company's current assets and its current liabilities. The excess of current assets over current liabilities is known as the company's *working capital*. The Gneiding Corporation has total current assets of $10,709,000 and current liabilities of $4,693,000. Its working capital is therefore $6,016,000. To convert this dollar value to a more meaningful measure, analysts divide current assets by current liabilities to arrive at the company's *current ratio*. Dividing Gneiding's current assets of $10,709,000 by its current liabilities of $4,693,000 gives a current ratio of 2.28 to 1. The company thus has $2.28 worth of current assets for each dollar of its current liabilities; its near-term obligations are covered 2.28 times. For the average manufacturing company, an acceptable current ratio is 2 to 1, so our sample corporation appears to be in good shape with respect to this standard.

A more severe test of a company's ability to meet its short-term obligations is its *quick asset ratio*. This is calculated by dividing quick assets by current liabilities. Gneiding's quick assets are $5,703,000 (cash + marketable securities + accounts receivable). Dividing these quick assets by current liabilities yields a quick asset ratio of 1.22 to 1 ($5,703,000 / $4,693,000 = 1.22). A quick asset ratio of 1 to 1 is considered acceptable, so Gneiding Corporation passes this test as well. The quick asset ratio is sometimes referred to as the *acid test ratio* or *liquidity ratio*.

Capitalization Ratios

The net worth portion of the balance sheet can be examined to determine the corporation's *capitalization ratios*. These ratios measure the relative amount of the company's capitalization represented by its common stock, preferred stock, and bonds. Gneiding's capitalization totals $19,522,000, consisting of bonds with a par value of $1,250,000, preferred stock with a par value of $1,235,000, and common stock worth a total of $17,037,000. Note that the common stock account is the total of three different figures: the common stock account ($3,865,000), capital surplus ($1,231,000), and retained earnings ($11,941,000). The company's bond ratio is 6.4% ($1,250,000 / $19,522,000), its preferred stock ratio is 6.3% ($1,235,000 / $19,522,000), and its common stock ratio is 87.3% ($17,037,000 / $19,522,000). This signifies that Gneiding has an extremely conservative capitalization. Companies with a fairly substantial portion of their capitalization represented by bonds or preferred stock are considered to be *highly leveraged*. Industrial companies with more than a third or so of their capitalization represented by debt (bonds) are considered to be in a leveraged situation. If such a company succeeds in carrying the debt and earning more with such a debt structure than it would otherwise, that's fine. But keep in mind that interest on bonds *must* be paid, unlike dividends on common stock, so large borrowings carry with them the risk of default.

Book Value

The amount that each share of common stock would be worth if the company were liquidated is known as its *book value*. It is the net asset value per share of common stock. The total worth of the common stock in this instance is $17,037,000 (see the preceding section). We must subtract the intangibles from this figure to reflect the fact that intangible assets wouldn't be worth anything if the company were liquidated, so our total net assets are $16,037,000 ($17,037,000 − $1,000,000). The Gneiding Corporation has 3,865,000 shares outstanding (refer to the balance sheet). Therefore its book value is $4.15 per share of common stock ($16,037,000 / 3,865,000).

THE INCOME STATEMENT

While a company's balance sheet reflects its assets, liabilities, and net worth at a specific time, its companion financial statement, the *income statement*, shows the company's income and expenses for an entire period, usually a quarter or a year. Also called the profit and loss statement or P & L, the income statement shows how much the company took in for sales and services, what its expenses were, and the amount of profit that was generated. A sample income statement for the Gneiding Corporation is presented.

GNEIDING CORPORATION
INCOME STATEMENT—JANUARY 1 TO DECEMBER 31, 20XX

Net Sales	$61,000,000
− Cost of Goods Sold	44,700,000
− Selling, General and Administrative Expenses	4,387,000
− Depreciation	1,855,000
= Operating Income (EBIT)	**10,058,000**
− Interest Paid on Outstanding Bonds	100,000
− Taxes	3,329,000
= Net Income	**6,629,000**
− Preferred Stock Dividends	86,450
= Net Earnings	**6,542,550**

Income Statement Analysis

The company's top line was $61,000,000 (*net sales*). *Cost of goods sold* includes raw materials and all other direct manufacturing costs. *Selling, general and administrative expenses* include commissions and salaries, advertising and promotion, and other nonfactory expenses. *Depreciation* is a non-cash expense, permitting the company to deduct, over time, the price it paid for fixed assets. The percentage of the company's sales that remains after these major expense categories is its *margin of profit*. Those expenses totaled $50,942,000, leaving $10,058,000 in operating income. Operating income ($10,058,000) divided by net sales ($61,000,000) gives Gneiding a margin of profit of 16.5%, substantially above average for manufacturing companies.

The company's *cash flow* is equal to its net income plus depreciation. With net income of $6,629,000 and depreciation of $1,855,000, Gneiding's cash flow is $8,484,000.

Earnings Per Share and Dividend Payout Ratio

One of the most important measurements of a company's operations is its earnings per share. *Earnings per share* represents the per-common-share profit after the company has paid all expenses, as well as dividends on its preferred stock. Gneiding's net earnings were $6,542,550. Since there are 3,865,000 common shares outstanding, the company's earnings per share were $1.69 ($6,542,550 / 3,865,000 = $1.69).

Presuming that the company is paying an annual dividend of $0.72 per share (a quarterly rate of $0.18 per share), Gneiding's *payout ratio* is 43%. This is the amount of the dividend expressed as a percentage of the earnings per share ($0.72 / $1.69 = 43%).

Current Yield and Price–Earnings Ratio

The *current yield* on Gneiding's common stock can be found by dividing the annual dividend on the stock by its current market price. Presuming a current market price of 32.50, the common stock's current yield is 2.2% ($0.72 / 32.50 = 2.2%).

A stock's *price–earnings ratio* (P/E) gives an indication of the relative expensiveness of a stock as compared with its earnings. It is calculated by dividing the current market price by the earnings per share. With a current market price of 32.50 and per-share earnings of $1.69, Gneiding's P/E ratio is 19.2 (32.50 / $1.69 = 19.2). Stocks with good growth prospects tend to have higher P/Es than mature issues.

TECHNICAL ANALYSIS

Also known as charting, *technical analysis* attempts to forecast future trends through a study of past price action and trading volume. Unlike fundamental analysis, this type of research is not concerned with a company's financial position. Many investors utilize technical analysis in conjunction with fundamental analysis, using the charting approach to *time* the purchases and sales of securities that they have selected through the more conventional method. Basically, the chartist believes that "what is past is prologue" and that the careful study of *past* price activity will allow one to predict *future* price activity. The chartist also pays attention to the volume of trading and the number of shares sold short.

The two principal charting methods are *bar charting* and *point-and-figure charting*. In bar charting, there is a vertical line for each day's trading that indicates that day's high, low, and closing trade prices. Point-and-figure charting uses a grid that compresses time and shows only price changes, up or down. The technical analyst carefully measures *trading ranges*, as it is particularly significant when a stock "breaks out" of a trading range. Chartists attempt to establish the level at which a stock seems to become attractive to buyers who consider that price a bargain. This is the *support level*, where *demand* comes into play. The upper end of a security's trading range, where sellers seem to *supply* so many shares that the stock doesn't move higher, is known as *resistance*. Some of the more common chart patterns are: head and shoulders, flag, pennant, saucer, and triangle. These recurring patterns are used to project future price trends.

SUMMARY

The two major schools of securities analysis are the fundamental and the technical. The former concerns itself with a study of balance sheets and income statements, earnings and dividends, and other information that demonstrate a company's business track record. Chartists focusing on technical analysis work almost exclusively with a security's past price movement and volume.

Fundamental analysts track a company's performance through an in-depth study of its financial statements, noting the current ratios and, even more important, the trend of such ratios. Major price moves often occur just after the release of a company's earnings report. The reports are eagerly awaited and investors react (and sometimes *over*react) when the reports are better or worse than the analytical community had anticipated.

Technical analysis is particularly useful when trying to establish a security's support and resistance levels, so as to establish the most effective price levels at which to enter stop orders. Chartists are often consulted by fundamental analysts when they are concerned with the proper pricing or timing of a prospective purchase or sale.

MULTIPLE-CHOICE QUIZ

1. Which of the following would be of interest to a technical analyst?
   a. earnings per share
   b. price–earnings ratio
   c. trading volume
   d. current ratio

2. The formula for cash flow is:
   a. Net Earnings – Operating Income
   b. Operating Income + Preferred Dividends
   c. Cost of Goods Sold – Selling, General and Administrative Expenses
   d. Net Income + Depreciation

3. An acceptable minimum quick asset ratio for a manufacturing company is:
   a. 1 to 1
   b. 2 to 1
   c. 1 to 2
   d. Manufacturing companies do not have quick assets or quick asset ratios.

4. A highly leveraged capitalization is indicated by:
   a. a large percentage of common stock
   b. a high payout ratio
   c. a relatively low book value
   d. a large amount of bonds outstanding

5. Earnings per share are calculated by dividing net earnings by:
   a. depreciation
   b. total capitalization
   c. outstanding shares
   d. cost of goods sold

PRACTICE EXERCISES

Use the balance sheet provided to answer questions 1 to 9. Calculate XYZ Manufacturing Corporation's:

1. quick assets

2. working capital

3. current ratio

4. liquidity ratio

5. capitalization

6. bond ratio

7. preferred stock ratio

8. common stock ratio

9. book value per common share

XYZ MANUFACTURING CORPORATION
BALANCE SHEET
DECEMBER 31, 20XX

Assets		Liabilities	
Cash	$ 50,000	Accounts Payable	$ 100,000
Marketable Securities	84,000	Notes Payable	85,000
Accounts Receivable	268,000	Accrued Expenses	95,000
Inventory	254,000	Accrued Taxes	70,000
Total Current Assets	$ 656,000	Total Current Liabilities	$ 350,000
Property, Plant, and Equipment	462,000	Bonds, 7% due 2025	250,000
		Total Liabilities	$ 600,000
		Net Worth	
Prepayments	27,000	Preferred Stock, $50 par	$ 50,000
		Common Stock, $25 par	100,000
		Paid-In Capital	50,000
Intangibles	30,000	Retained Earnings	375,000
		Total Net Worth	575,000
Total Assets	$1,175,000	Total Liabilities and Net Worth	$1,175,000

Use the income statement provided to answer questions 10 to 17. Calculate all ratios and percentages to one decimal place, rounded appropriately. Calculate all dollar-denominated answers to the nearest full cent. Marobeth Corporation common stock is trading at 52.75 and the company is paying an annual cash dividend of $0.75 on the common stock. There are 900,000 common shares outstanding. Calculate Marobeth Corporation's:

10. expense ratio

11. margin of profit

12. cash flow

13. earnings per share

14. payout ratio

15. current yield on common stock

16. price–earnings ratio

17. book value per common share

MAROBETH CORPORATION
INCOME STATEMENT—1/1/XX TO 12/31/XX

	Net Sales	16,500,000
−	Cost of Goods Sold	11,788,000
−	Selling, General and Administrative Expenses	1,413,000
−	Depreciation	630,000
	Operating Income	2,669,000
+	Other Income	68,500
	Total Income (Earnings Before Interest and Taxes)	2,737,500
−	Interest	402,600
−	Taxes	793,866
	Net Income	1,541,034
−	Preferred Stock Dividends	59,060
	Net Earnings	1,481,974

MULTIPLE-CHOICE ANSWERS AND EXPLANATIONS

1. **c.** The other choices would be of interest to the fundamental analyst.

2. **d.** Cash flow is, essentially, the amount of actual cash the company had left from its operations after expenses but before paying dividends. We add back depreciation because it is a non-cash expense.

3. **a.** A quick asset ratio of 1 to 1 indicates that a company has as much in its cash, marketable securities, and inventory accounts (its quick assets) as it has current liabilities. Companies that have easily collectible receivables (such as utilities) can work with a much thinner ratio such as .9 or .8 to 1.

4. **d.** A relatively large amount of debt in a company's capital structure marks it as highly leveraged. While there is no precise figure, a bond ratio of 40% or more indicates a leveraged situation. Keep in mind that while the interest a company pays on its debt is deductible—preferred and common stock dividends are not deductible—the interest must be paid to avoid the penalties of default, which might include the repossession of assets pledged as collateral.

5. **c.** The correct formula is to divide net earnings (the company's bottom line) by the number of common shares outstanding. (Include shares that are authorized, issued, and outstanding, but do not include authorized but unissued shares or treasury stock.)

ANSWERS TO PRACTICE EXERCISES

1. $402,000

   Quick assets = Current assets − Inventory

   Quick assets = $656,000 − $254,000

   Quick assets = $402,000

2. $306,000

   Working capital = Current assets − Current liabilities

   Working capital = $656,000 − $350,000

   Working capital = $306,000

3. 1.9 to 1

   Current ratio = Current assets / Current liabilities

   Current ratio = $656,000 / $350,000

   Current ratio = 1.9 to 1

4. 1.1 to 1

   Liquidity ratio = Quick assets / Current liabilities

   Liquidity ratio = $402,000 / $350,000

   Liquidity ratio = 1.1 to 1

5. $825,000

   Capitalization = Funded debt + Net worth

   Capitalization = $250,000 + $575,000

   Capitalization = $825,000

6. 30.3%

   Bond ratio = Funded debt / Capitalization

   Bond ratio = $250,000 / $825,000

   Bond ratio = 30.3%

7. 6.1%

   Preferred stock ratio = Preferred stock / Capitalization

   Preferred stock ratio = $50,000 / $825,000

   Preferred stock ratio = 6.1%

8. 63.6%

   Common stock ratio = Common stockholders' equity / Capitalization

   Common stock ratio = $525,000 / $825,000

   Common stock ratio = 63.6%

9. $123.75

   Book value = Common stockholders' equity – Intangibles / Number of common shares outstanding

   Book value = ($525,000 – $30,000) / 4,000

   Book value = $495,000 / 4,000 = $123.75

   Note: The number of common shares outstanding can be derived by dividing the total par value of the outstanding common stock ($100,000) by the par value ($25).

10. 83.8%

    Expense ratio = Expenses / Net sales

    Expense ratio = $13,831,000 / $16,500,000

    Expense ratio = 83.8%

11. 16.2%

    Margin of profit = Operating income / Net sales

    Margin of profit = $2,669,000 / $16,500,000

    Margin of profit = 16.2%

    Note: The expense ratio and the margin of profit should add to 100%: 83.8% + 16.2% = 100%.

12. $2,171,034

    Cash flow = Net income + Depreciation

    Cash flow = $1,541,034 + $630,000

    Cash flow = $2,171,034

13. $1.65

    Earnings per share = Net earnings / Number of common shares outstanding

    Earnings per share = $1,481,974 / 900,000

    Earnings per share = $1.65

14. 45.5%

Payout ratio = Annual dividend / Earnings per share

Payout ratio = $0.75 / $1.65

Payout ratio = 45.5%

15. 1.4%

Current yield = Annual dividend / Current price

Current yield = $0.75 / 52.75

Current yield = 1.4%

16. 32 to 1

Price–Earnings ratio = Current price / Earnings per share

Price–Earnings ratio = 52.75 / 1.65

Price–Earnings ratio = 32 to 1

17. Cannot be determined from the information presented.

Book value per common share is derived by dividing common stockholders' equity (reduced by intangibles) by the number of common shares outstanding. You do not have sufficient information to calculate it, as that requires information from the company's balance sheet as well.

About the Author

William A. Rini, former Senior Vice President of the New York Institute of Finance—the world's foremost financial training organization—created the popular four-week program for international financial executives, the United States Capital Markets Seminar. He designed customized training programs for the Korea Securities Training Institute, the Mexican Stock Exchange, the Taiwan Security Dealers Association, and the Saudi Arabian Monetary Agency. His international programs have been attended by financial professionals from more than 135 different countries. He remains an active instructor, consultant, and author, and he lectures to financial professionals both in the United States and abroad.

Mr. Rini has addressed audiences from many of the major commercial banking and investment banking institutions in America, and has presented and moderated seminars for the American Management Association across the United States; for the International Bank for Reconstruction and Development in Kenya and The People's Republic of China, and for central banks, capital market authorities, securities exchanges, and financial training institutions in Hungary, India, Indonesia, Japan, Kuwait, Mexico, and Saudi Arabia. He has lectured to audiences from the New York Stock Exchange, the American Stock Exchange, the Securities and Exchange Commission, the National Association of Securities Dealers, and the Nasdaq Stock Market.

Mr. Rini developed the qualifying examinations for securities salespersons, underwriters, and investment advisors licensed by the Indonesian Capital Market Authority, and served as advisor with respect to their grading, implementation, and administration.

He has authored a book on stock-brokerage mathematics, is co-author of a text to prepare salespersons for Investment Company/Variable Contract licensing, and is a contributing editor to a text on personal investing.

Index